Beyond the Midnight Mountains

Christopher Charlton – or Kipper for short – has an unusual side to h
His toys come to life! Th
Noah and his Ark
toy soldier
com
Tin
the
river
bedpo
tops a
range Midnight
Mounta

Ever s discovered the world of his toys, Kipper has wanted to go beyond the Midnight Mountains, but the toys have always stopped him. But when Lady Precious Pearl and her little green dragon arrive on the scene, everything blows apart and Kipper and the toys, with the help of Sir Roland and King Arthur's sword Excalibur, find themselves pitted against the wicked magician Abu Nazir and his apprentice Shadow in a fight to the death to regain Aladdin's magic lamp.

A funny and engaging story which will capture the imagination of children of 8 and over.

BEYOND THE MIDNIGHT MOUNTAINS

Frank Charles

Illustrations by Lynn Smith

A Hippo Book
Scholastic Publications Limited
London

Scholastic Publications, Ltd.
161 Fulham Road, London, SW3 6SW, England

Scholastic Book Services,
50 West 44th Street, New York, 10036, NY, USA

Scholastic Tab Publications Ltd,
123 Newkirk Road, Richmond Hill, Ontario L4C 3G5, Canada

H. J. Ashton Co. Pty, Ltd,
Box 579, Gosford, New South Wales, Australia

H. J. Ashton Co. Pty, Ltd,
9–11 Fairfax Avenue, Penrose, Auckland, New Zealand

First published by Andersen Press Ltd., 1977
Published by Scholastic Publications Ltd., 1980
Second impression, April 1980

Made and printed in Great Britain by
Hazell Watson & Viney Ltd
Aylesbury, Bucks
Set in Bembo

Contents

To my wife, Margaret; my children,
Chris, John and Jill, and to Peter Street,
who have all shown so much faith
in this story.

1 The Magic Time

This is the story of an adventure that happened to me last Christmas Eve.

Before going any further I suppose I ought to introduce myself properly. My full name is Christopher Andrew Jonathan Aloysius Alexander Charlton, but no one wants to be lumbered with a mouthful like that, do they? Everyone calls me 'Kipper', except schoolteachers and the curate and I don't count them. I have a freckled face, a loud voice and ears that stick out like cream jug handles.

I live in a large, red-bricked house in London and my playroom is at the top of it in an attic room with a skylight and a box window. No one else in the family wanted it because the ceiling slants down on one side and this means that grown-ups have to walk round with their necks askew and they don't like that at all. Grown-ups are born fussers and they hate being at all uncomfortable so they offered the room to me and I grabbed it.

Oh I *love* that room. I have my bed with the patchwork quilt in one corner under the slanting bit of roof and I keep all my favourite books up there.

This adventure started off very quietly. I was kneeling on the landing outside the playroom and I'd just finished wrapping up a rather special Christmas present for my mum, who is small and dark and has a rather sad face although she's quite a cheerful person really.

Outside the house it was raining. The raindrops were tap dancing all over the roof and on the glass of the skylight. An icy cold wind was whistling round the house and then dying away with a melancholy gurgle down the streets and alleyways.

I was glad I was inside in the warm. I like Christmas. It's exciting thinking about all the presents you're going to get, and the turkey and roast spuds you're going to chomp your way through, and all the jellies and trifle and Christmas pudding and mincepies you intend to consume. I like Christmas because I like eating.

I also knew that Dad was making plans to take me to see a pantomime. I heard him talking to Mum about it when he thought I wasn't listening, but I haven't got big, flappy, stuck-out ears for nothing. I flapped them, and gathered he was going to take me to see *Aladdin and his Wonderful Lamp* at a posh West End theatre. I felt shivery inside with anticipation.

'Kipper!' called a voice from downstairs. 'Bedtime!'

'Yes, Mum,' I yelled back. 'In a minute.'

I scrawled out her name on the label and tied it to the box I'd wrapped and then I crept forward to the attic door and opened it a tiny, weeny little crack. I pushed the oblong box inside and then I sat back on my heels and waited for reactions.

No one noticed it at first. But I knew they were all up and moving about in there – Benjie, Teddy, Old Man Noah and his animals. I always know. I can hear them rustling and chattering. It's very interesting, sometimes, to watch them when they don't know I'm there, so I bent forward and put my eye to the crack in the door and peered into the playroom.

Benjie, the toy soldier, was up on the window sill with his nose pressed to the glass surveying the weather with a gloomy expression on his face.

Teddy Bear was sitting propped up against the gangway of the ark, placidly smoking his pipe.

Old Man Noah was fussing about on the deck of the ark and falling over ropes and pulleys and dropping his brass telescope every few minutes. Everything was peaceful and quite normal.

I don't remember exactly when it was that I knew that

my toys had a life of their own, but I think it was when I was much younger, very small and in bed with mumps or measles. I think it was mumps because I remember I had a sore throat and couldn't talk above a hoarse whisper.

I opened my eyes one morning and there I saw Benjie sitting next to Ted at the end of my bed and they were talking to each other. I was so astonished I stayed there, quite still, and I listened, instead of butting in as I usually do. They were talking about *me*.

'Just look at him,' said Benjie, 'lying there fast asleep. Looks like a proper little angel, don't he?'

Benjie is a right little London Cockney, just like me. He wears a red jacket with white buttons and a Corporal's stripes on one arm. His trousers are black and very neatly pressed, but his busby's got a bit moth-eaten over the years. It keeps falling off. Underneath it he's got black spiky hair that sticks up in great surprise all over his head.

'Indeed he does,' replied Teddy in a deep brown rumbly voice, and he swivelled his tufty eyebrows in my direction. 'No one would think that such an angelic little boy, while he's asleep, could bear such a distinct resemblance to Attila the Hun when he's awake.'

I was insulted and fascinated, all in one go. Teddy was talking just as I'd always imagined he'd talk. Deep, slow and solemn, as if he never said anything he hadn't had a good long think about first.

He's a middle-aged Teddy Bear and I noticed, for the first time, that *he's* a trifle battered round the edges too. One ear had come unstitched and there were bald patches on his fur as if some careless child had bashed him around rather a lot. I wondered who the child could possibly be. Then I realized! It was *me*!

Benjie rubbed his nose and squiggled it sideways.

'Large as life and twice as irritating, that's our bossy boots, but I hope he gets better soon, 'cos I don't like to see him lying there so quiet, with a face like an overblown football. I'll be glad when he's better, even though it *is* like living with a permanent earthquake on the premises. *But*, when he is up and prancing around again, we've gotta be careful, Ted. We're the guards we are; you, me, and daffy Old Man Noah and we gotta protect him. We gotta see to it he doesn't meet nothing too dangerous while he's too small to handle it.'

I struggled up in my bed and they both froze, stiff and solid, and refused to move or talk while I was awake.

It was a long time before they trusted me and learned to carry on whether I was awake or asleep. At first they always froze whenever I came clumping into the play-room, but I knew they could hear me even if they pretended to be deaf, dumb and silly, and, gradually, over the months that followed my illness, I managed to get them to relax and play with me properly. Sometimes they let me come right into their world and when that happens I call it the 'Magic Time'.

Everything in the attic room suddenly grows larger. The ceiling is miles above me and the walls stretch away into the distance and they seem melty, as if they were going to dissolve, and when they do, everything else changes.

The carpet, for instance. It's just a tatty old green carpet with a blue border. Mum got it from her deaf auntie in Swindon. That's the auntie with false teeth that click and keep on falling out when she talks. The carpet becomes a meadow with real grass and the blue border becomes a river winding away to the sea. I always stick the ark on the blue bit so that it's not stuck on shore when the Magic Time comes. I know Old Man Noah, and he'd never get it afloat if I didn't take that small precaution.

The bedposts start sprouting branches and leaves and they become four tall trees and Benjie's castle is as big and as solid as the Tower of London.

The rooftops of dull old Peckham Rye change too. They become a range of coal black mountains with snow, and glaciers and all the trimmings and they surround us on all sides so there's no way through them.

From the very beginning I wanted to explore beyond

them, but, somehow, Benjie and Teddy and Noah always manage to head me off. They keep on saying that it's dangerous beyond the Midnight Mountains and they are quite convinced that it's their job to keep me out of trouble. As if they could! No one has ever managed to keep me out of trouble and I was determined to break out somehow. That's what this story is all about.

I pushed the playroom door so that I could see a wider section of the floor and I wiggled the oblong box sideways.

No one had noticed it yet, but, sooner or later, they would and I wanted to see what they'd do about this mysterious intruder into their world. Of course, I knew what was inside the box, but they didn't and I suppose that gave me an unfair advantage really.

Benjie turned away from the window and glanced down at Teddy Bear.

'Luvvly weather we're not havin',' he remarked casually. 'Raining cats and dogs. Put one foot outside and you'll step into a poodle.'

He chuckled. Then he giggled.

'I say,' he said. 'That's rather good. Did you get it, Ted? Cats, dogs, poodle. Don't you think that's funny?'

Teddy Bear turned his head very slowly. He sucked his pipe. He puffed out a long stream of smoke.

'No,' he said flatly.

Benjie straightened his busby, pulled down his red jacket and picked up his rifle. 'Ah well. Can't win 'em all,' he muttered philosophically.

He climbed down from the window ledge via two chairs and a Tin-Tin book and marched stumpily across the floor towards the ark.

'NOAAAAAAH!' he shouted. 'What's the time?'

Old Man Noah trotted across the deck and poked his head over the rail. 'About eight bells,' he beamed. 'Let's say seven bells and a tinkle, eh?'

Benjie put his hands on his hips and glared at him.

'What's that in English?' he demanded. 'I can't speak arithmetic. Never did understand them bells of your'n Noah.'

'*Don't* you?' said Old Man Noah, and a delighted beam swept across his craggy old face. 'Neither do I! Come to think of it I don't understand all that "Hard a port and luff to starboard" stuff either. Baffling.'

Old Man Noah is the Captain of the ark. He's a baldheaded old coot with mild blue eyes and he has a very big nose. He says it's not so much a nose as a peninsula attached to a mainland of face and he's just about right. I like Old Man Noah. Everyone likes Old Man Noah even though he's as daffy as a bedbug and totally accident prone.

He tucked his telescope under his arm and bumbled his way down the gangway to join Teddy and Benjie. Halfway down he tripped over a loose plank and landed on his nose.

'Drat that plank,' he said, scrambling to his feet and pulling his long robes down over his skinny legs. 'I meant to mend it but I lost me hammer. One minute I was waving it about enthusiastically and the next, gone, absolutely.'

It was at that moment that Benjie noticed the mysterious box. He stared across the room at it. His eyes bulged out like organ stops and he frowned.

'Hey,' he said. 'What's that?'

Old Man Noah followed the direction of his quivering finger.

'It's a box,' he said, helpfully.

Benjie threw his eyeballs all around the room and made gurgling noises in his throat. 'Why don't you jack yerself up and change your head?' he said irritably. 'I can see it's a box fer meself. But who does it belong to and what's it doing here and all that jazz?'

Teddy Bear knocked out the dottle from his pipe on the newly painted gangway and scratched his stomach and waved his eyebrows about and then, after due thought and consideration, came out with a statement.

'Since it is Christmas Eve, and at Christmas people give each other presents, I think we can safely assume that it is a present.'

Benjie looked worried. His eyebrows shot up into his busby and then came down again by parachute.

'A present?' he whispered. 'Fer Christopher? Oh Lor', I wonder if it's an Action Man.'

'A what?' said Teddy.

'An Action Man,' said Benjie miserably. 'One o' them new-fangled toy soldiers. They talk outa the sides of their mouths and chew gum and have all the latest equipment. Kids luv 'em.'

Teddy looked at Old Man Noah. Old Man Noah looked at Teddy.

'Why on earth should it be an Action Man?' they asked in unison.

'Because I'm too old-fashioned, that's why,' said Benjie. 'They're gonna replace me. I can see it all. I'm no good any more, wiv me old-fashioned musket and suchlike. I'm gonna be pensioned off and I'll have ter sit in an old toy soldiers' home maundering on about old times. Look at me! Past me best. Over the hill and down the other side.'

I must admit I felt a bit guilty when I heard him say that, because, as a matter of fact, I had been dropping hints to Dad that I'd like an Action Man for Christmas. Honestly, I'd no idea that it would upset old Benjie like that.

'*Benjie*!' growled Teddy. 'Shut up. You talk too much.'

'Me?' howled Benjie. 'I don't.'

'Well, let us say your silences are too short,' said Teddy firmly. 'Of *course* they're not going to replace you. Why, you're one of the best guards Kipper ever had. They won't replace you with an Action Man, you silly little toy soldier you. Modern muck. How could an Action Man guard our Kipper, eh? No tradition.'

It's funny, but that was more or less what Dad had said when I hinted that I'd like one for Christmas.

'There's a label on that box,' Teddy went on. 'I suggest you read it.'

Benjie sniffed. 'It's nice of yer to try and comfort me,' he said. 'But it's no use. I can just feel an Action Man in that box, screaming ter get out. All day I've had one o' them watchermercallems, a premonition. Something is about to happen and I'm not gonna like it. My stomach's bin chuntering about like a concertina with the staggers.'

'Noah,' said Teddy. 'Read that label.'

Old Man Noah trotted obligingly across the room and squinted up at the label. 'It says – er – CHRISTOPHER FROM LOVE WITH MUMMY TO,' he announced.

Then he blushed. 'Sorry – it's upside down. Silly me.'

He stood on his head and read it the right way up this time. 'TO MUMMY WITH LOVE FROM CHRISTOPHER.'

Teddy thumped Benjie on the back. 'There, you see,' he growled. 'It's a present from Kipper to his mother. If he's bought her an Action Man I shall be most surprised and she'll be furious.'

Benjie looked tremendously relieved. 'I'm reprieved!' he shouted. 'Teddy! I luvs yer, you animated hearthrug you. Yippee!' And he grabbed Teddy by the paws and started to revolve all round the room. In the middle of this routine he broke off and stared at the box again.

'I wonder what *is* in that box?' he said.

I decided it was time I put in an appearance so I pushed open the attic door and strolled in very casually. Teddy, Benjie and Old Man Noah sprang to attention and arranged themselves into a straight line, more or less.

'At ease, men,' I said, and rummaged under my pillow for my pyjamas. I pulled them out and began to change ready for bed so there wouldn't be a fuss when Mum came upstairs to check. I pulled on my striped pyjama trousers and tied the cord and then I crouched down near Benjie.

'What's the chances of an adventure when the Magic Time begins?' I asked.

He moved away from Teddy and Old Man Noah and cocked an eye up at the skylight.

'Can't go out. It's raining.'

'Course we can,' I wheedled. 'We can go in the ark, can't we? That was built for rain.'

Benjie sat himself down on a nearby Lego brick and pursed up his mouth at me. 'Do you think that's altogether wise?' he said softly. 'After all, there is Old Man Noah. Nicest chap in the world o' course, but hardly the Captain I'd choose for any ship I was going ter be aboard. Ever seen his compass? It's the only one in the

world with North, South, East, West and "Blimey we're lost" on it.'

'Benjie,' I said. 'You're an old fussy britches. I want an adventure. We haven't had a really good one in ages and ages.'

I heard Mum's footsteps on the stairs so I plonked myself into my bed and made a great do about yawning when she came in. She kissed me, said goodnight and beamed fondly and did all the usual things that mums do, and then she went away, closing the door behind her.

So I got out of bed again and crouched down beside Benjie. He was looking cunning.

'Tell you what,' he said. 'You do something fer me and then mebbe I'll be able to do something for you. Fair doos?'

I grinned to myself. I could guess what was coming next.

'What do you want me to do?'

'Tell me,' he said, 'what's in that box over there?'

'Oh *that*!' I said carelessly. 'Nothing much. Just a present for Mum. Dad chose it really. Said she'd like it. Blowed if I'd want it, but mums seems to want all sorts of odd things, don't they?'

'Can we have a little peek at it?' asked Benjie. He's as curious as a magpie.

'Can if you like,' I shrugged. 'But don't blame me if you think it's very dull when you do see it.'

Benjie jerked his thumb towards Teddy and the pair of them walked across the room to the box while Old Man Noah hovered in the middle distance and dropped his telescope in his excitement.

They looked so small down there, tramping round the oblong box and untying the ribbon. I have to crouch right down or lie flat on my stomach if I want to talk to them properly. I must seem like a giant.

Benjie pulled back the gay wrapping paper and then lugged open the box lid as if he was pulling a door on a hinge. He and Teddy peeped inside.

Then he spun round and stared up at me, his eyes blinking rapidly.

'You call that *dull*?' he yelled.

Inside the box there was a tiny ivory statuette of a Chinese girl. She was a dancer and she had a little green dragon carved out of jade crouching at her feet. She carried a small ivory fan.

I suppose it was a very pretty piece of carving but I wasn't terribly excited about it myself. It was only a statuette of a girl after all, and everybody knows how useless girls are.

I pointed this out to Benjie and he began to get really excited. He rolled his eyes about and his eyebrows looped the loop and then he waved his arms like a demented windmill. I'd never seen him get so worked up.

'She's beautiful!' he said. 'She's lovely. She – she's the most beautifullest, loveliest girl I've ever seen.'

Teddy tapped him on the shoulder.

'Calm down, Benjie,' he said soothingly. 'Remember that Kipper is very young.'

'I don't care how young he is,' snorted Benjie. 'Surely even a clodhopping boy with the soul of a dustcart can see that she's gorgeous, she's wonderful, she – she – she . . .'

Benjie broke off in mid rhapsody and peered right into the box at the statuette.

'She's alive,' he whispered. 'Look Ted – there's tears trickling down her face. She's one of us.'

Teddy bent forward and inspected the Chinese girl's face and nodded.

'She must've bin enchanted by a wicked wizard or an evil magician,' said Benjie. 'We gotta help her Ted. We gotta help her.'

I wriggled closer and had a look at her for myself. Benjie was quite right. Two huge brown eyes looked at me from out of that frozen ivory face, and tears were trickling down her cheeks and splashing on to her ornamental fan.

I was a bit shaken I must admit, but I wasn't going to let anyone know it. 'Girls are always grizzling about something,' I said casually. 'I should know. My sister's always howling her head off over nothing.'

But Benjie wasn't listening.

'Noah,' he said. 'We've got ter do something.'

'Oh dear,' said Old Man Noah, and twiddled with his telescope till it came apart in his hands. 'I'm not much good at magic. Never was. I pull hats out of rabbits. Frightful mistake.'

His face cleared. 'Wait a bit,' he said. 'I know who can help us. The wife. She knows all about everything. I'll go aboard and ask her.'

'You do that small thing,' said Benjie, and then he stood by the box and stared in at the Chinese girl with his mouth open again.

I was beginning to get restless. It was all very interesting but I wanted to get going on an adventure and I couldn't while they were fussing about round this statuette.

I can have lots of fun just being with them in the attic

room, and hearing them talk and watching the things they do, but I can't enter into their world completely unless they allow it. I don't know how it happens, mind you. That's one of their secrets. But I do know that I can't go off with them on an adventure until the Magic Time comes, and it never comes when I want it to come, but only when they allow it.

Old Man Noah came dashing back and fell down the gangway again.

'I've got the answer,' he said. 'The wife knew. Wonderful woman, the wife. Absolutely terrifying of course, but wonderful.'

'Well?' demanded Benjie. 'What do we do?'

'Kiss her of course,' said Noah. 'Works wonders. Brings 'em round in no time. Sleeping princesses, maidens, damsels, all sorts. Never fails.'

'Who is going ter do it?' asked Benjie.

There was a soupy silence and it seemed to spread all over the attic room. We all looked straight at poor old Benjie. He looked this way and that way.

'Wh – why are you all looking at *me*?' he squeaked.

Teddy Bear clumped him on the shoulder. 'Brace up, Benjie,' he murmured encouragingly. 'It'll have to be you. No one else qualifies. Noah is too old. Kipper is much too young and while I might venture to cut a swathe with a lady bruin I doubt if my charms would have much effect on a comatose Chinese maiden. You're the only one left. The classic solution, of course, is a handsome prince but we're rather short on handsome princes at the moment so it'll have to be done by a pug-nosed toy soldier who's all mouth and no trousers.'

'Thanks very much,' said Benjie.

'Go on,' said Teddy. 'Have a go. *Kiss her!*'

It's a funny thing but whenever Teddy Bear gives an order like that, we all jump to obey him, even me. Before Benjie had time to think he found he'd jumped forward and planted a timid but quite definite kiss on the statuette's cold lips.

The effect was instantaneous. The tiny green dragon at her feet uncurled itself and stretched its wings while the Chinese girl herself stepped forward out of the box and bowed and smiled radiantly upon one and all.

'The enchantment is broken,' she said in a clear high voice. 'My thanks to you all.'

And, as she said it, I became aware that the room was growing larger and larger and larger and the carpet under my feet was changing into soft, prickly grass. The Magic Time had arrived.

Shadow's Diary – Interruption 1

Unbeknown to Christopher and his friends there was, far, far away on the other side of the Midnight Mountains, a palace which belonged to a wicked magician.

On the left wing of that palace there was a tall, white tower. Inside the tower there was a circular room with a balcony running right round the outside. The room was bare except for a table and a high stool. On the table there was a magical, far-seeing crystal ball. On the stool there was a tall, slender, handsome young apprentice wizard who had pale green skin and lovely purple hair and was altogether beautiful except for the fact that his good looks were marred by having one, slightly bloodshot, eyeball. But then anybody might have a bloodshot eyeball if they had to gaze into a crystal ball for hours and hours and hours on end.

As the Chinese girl stepped out of the box in the attic room, the tall, slender, handsome young apprentice wizard straightened himself up, rubbed his hands together and cracked all his knuckles one after the other and said gleefully, 'He won't like this. Ooooh no, my dear master won't like this at all. How delightful it will be to be the very first with really bad news!'

He chuckled maliciously and cracked all his knuckles again so they sounded like pistol shots echoing round the tower room.

2 Lady Precious Pearl

What really happens during the Magic Time is that I get smaller, but it doesn't feel like that. It feels as if everyone is growing up to my size when really it's the other way round and I am shrinking down to theirs. It gave me a bit of a shock when I realized it, like the time I thought the train was moving and it wasn't. It was the train on the next railway track.

Teddy winked at me.

'Definitely *not* an Action Man,' he said in my ear. 'But trouble all the same, Kipper. My whiskers are twitching and my whiskers never twitch for nothing.'

And that's true too. Whenever Teddy's whiskers begin to twitch it's a sign that danger of one sort or another is near and we've all learned never to ignore Teddy's warnings.

Benjie was still staring at the Chinese girl like a thunderstruck codfish and it was obvious to me that no one was going to get any sense out of him till he'd got over it. I don't understand the effect that girls seem to have on normally sensible men but there it is. Everyone says I'll understand it *one* day.

'What is your name?' I asked politely.

'My name is Lady Precious Pearl,' she replied, and bowed.

'I'm Kipper,' I said. 'You'd better come aboard the ark and tell us how you came to be enchanted and all that jazz.'

'Thank you,' she said. 'I am most honoured.'

The little green dragon flew up in the air and perched itself on her shoulder. It looked back at me and winked a golden eyelid and suddenly I wanted, desperately, to have a little green dragon that would perch on my shoulder.

Benjie offered Lady Precious Pearl his arm and gallantly escorted her up the gangway and into the ark.

Teddy struck a match and lit his pipe and waggled his tufty eyebrows at me. 'Kipper,' he said. 'I suspect that this is the beginning of an adventure.'

'About time too,' I said, feelingly.

Old Man Noah trotted up alongside. 'I hate adventures,' he said. 'Why they made me a sailor I'll never know. I'd have been so much happier as a harbour master.'

'Why?' I asked.

'No one,' he said simply, 'has ever sunk a harbour.'

Teddy and I followed him up the gangway and we all gathered together below decks in my cosy little cabin. I lit the hurricane lamp and pulled out a chair for Precious Pearl while everyone else crowded inside and perched themselves on the bunk, or wherever else they could find. I knelt on the floor next to the little green dragon and smiled at it hopefully.

The little green dragon blinked at me and polished its wings with one paw, just like a cat washing its fur.

'Hello, dragon,' I said.

'Greetings, small mortal,' it replied politely.

It had a high, clear, piping voice and sounded very grown up even though it was only a few inches long and could have perched on my shoulder just as easily as it sat on Precious Pearl.

I looked round the cabin. We were all there. Benjie was still gazing entranced at the Chinese girl.

Teddy was sitting on the floor with his back against the bulkhead and he was fiddling vaguely with his pipe and tobacco pouch again.

'Do you mind if I smoke?' he growled gruffly. 'You won't start opening the porthole and waving your arms about and coughing pointedly will you?'

'Be my guest,' I said. 'I rather like the smell of the muck actually.'

I wiggled my nose at the little green dragon. The little dragon grinned, and wiggled its nose right back at me. We were getting on famously. I felt very happy.

'Tell us your story,' I said to Lady Precious Pearl. 'How come you got yourself enchanted, and all that?'

She flicked her fan backwards and forwards for a few seconds and then smiled. She had a nice smile and she wasn't bad looking for a mere girl.

'My name is Lady Precious Pearl,' she repeated, 'and I am a woman of the western hills of Cathay.'

'Luvvly name, Precious Pearl,' breathed Benjie.

'Thank you,' she dimpled at him. 'But I am most unimportant person in myself. Although I come from most distinguished family, it is always the little twigs that do the most rustling on every family tree. I am on a quest. I seek a certain magic lamp.'

That sounded interesting.

'A magic lamp,' I said, butting in as usual. 'Do you

mean a magic lamp like in Aladdin, with a genie and so on and so forth?'

'Not merely like,' she corrected me gently, 'identical. It is the same lamp. I am the great, great grand-daughter of the famous Allah U Dhinn. It is my task to get back the lamp from the wicked magician Abu Nazir who stole it by a trick from Aladdin.'

I frowned.

'In the book I read at school Aladdin got the lamp back himself.'

The Chinese girl nodded. 'Many things in books that are not true in real life,' she said. 'That was happy ending stuck on the end of the story to make people feel good. In real life happy endings are sometimes harder to attain. Abu Nazir still holds the lamp and it is my appointed task to get it back again if I can.'

I patted the little green dragon on the head. He butted his scaly little snout against the palm of my hand.

'Hey!' I said to Benjie and Teddy and Old Man Noah. 'That'd be a real adventure, wouldn't it? To go and search for a magic lamp?'

'A most dangerous adventure,' said Lady Precious Pearl very quietly. 'You would be opposing the mind and will of Abu Nazir and he is an enemy both dark and deadly.'

'I'm not scared,' I said, and stroked the little green dragon's wings.

'You've never met a wicked magician,' said Teddy. 'Very tricky things, magicians.'

'Pooey!' I said scornfully. 'Are you scared, Benjie?'

'Petrified,' he said promptly. 'But I'll do it if it'll help Lady Precious Pearl.'

'How about you, Noah?' I asked.

'You mean I have a choice?' he said.

'No, not really,' I answered. 'Is the ark ready for sea, Noah?'

'Yes,' he said, and added, 'unfortunately.'

'Then let's pull up the anchor and get going.'

We all trooped up on deck and Old Man Noah started blowing his whistle and shouting orders so, of course, there was instant chaos.

Mickey and Mookey, his two little monkeys, shot up into the rigging and dropped the mainsail. It came hurtling down at about 300 kilometres an hour.

For once, Old Man Noah saw it coming and stepped neatly sideways, but he stepped into a coil of moving rope that was running through the capstan and it promptly wrapped itself all round him and tied him to the mainmast.

'Oh well,' he said. 'At least I can't fall down a hatchway, can I?'

We untied him and gradually some sort of order came creeping out of the general pandemonium.

The sail rose in the air and billowed out as the wind filled it. Two baby elephants hauled up the anchor and it came up out of the water with a soft sploosh, dripping with seaweed and a surprised lobster.

Old Man Noah grabbed the tiller and swung it over to port.

Slowly, gracefully, the ark turned and sailed straight up on to the shore. And there it stuck. I went and told Old Man Noah his fortune at the top of my voice for about five minutes.

Benjie suggested that Lady Precious Pearl should tell us her story properly to fill in the time.

'It is rather a long story,' she said.

'It'll be rather a long time before the tide turns,' he chuckled. 'Until then we're stuck on this mudbank good and proper.'

'Then gather round and incline your illustrious and well-shaped ears towards me and I'll tell you the story of my life and of my quest.'

She sat herself down on a bollard in the well deck and the animals, all chattering and giggling, sat round her in a semi-circle. Benjie came and sat one side of me and Teddy plonked himself down on the other while Old Man Noah, who was in disgrace, hid himself behind the capstan. The little green dragon fluttered its wings and flew across the deck and perched itself on my shoulder. I've never been so happy in my life.

It snuggled down and whispered in my left ear, 'I shall sleep. I already know the story and while it is most enthralling narrative to one who has not heard it before, I prefer taking dragon nap.'

I felt its claws digging gently into my shoulder and its head rubbing against my ear and then it began, very softly and quietly, to snore. It made a buzzing noise like a contented bumble bee.

Lady Precious Pearl waited until all the whispering and snuffling among her audience had stopped and when we were all gazing at her expectantly she began to speak.

She was quite right. It *was* a very long story and, as a matter of fact, she told it to us on and off all through the voyage.

She'd been born in a little village with a blue pagoda, and she was the great, great grand-daughter of Allah U Dhinn. She was also the seventh daughter of a seventh daughter which meant that she had six elder sisters and that must be terrible. I've only got one sister and believe me it's quite enough. Precious Pearl told us there was supposed to be something magical about being a seventh daughter of a seventh daughter and I didn't argue because I don't know enough about magic. Her adventures started when she was very young because some Mongolian bandits raided the village and carried her off into the mountains so she actually grew up in a secluded valley surrounded by robbers until she was old enough to escape. Not that escaping did her much good because she got lost in the mountains and had to take shelter in a cave and it was in that cave that she met a huge golden dragon.

Lady Precious Pearl didn't give a loud shriek and run away when she saw this huge golden dragon; she bowed politely and stayed in the cave with it for weeks. This particular dragon was her special guardian and helper and it was she who sent her out on the quest to get the magic lamp of power away from Abu Nazir, the wicked magician. In order to help her the dragon gave her two gifts. One was a bag of jewels which was useful because she could buy food, but the other was a most peculiar present. It was a large, oval, green egg. She must have looked very strange walking up to the walls of Peking with a bag of jewels in one hand and a huge green egg tucked under one arm.

The egg hatched out later on and became the little green dragon snoring on my shoulder and he was her constant companion in all her travels as she searched from the steaming jungles of Burma up to the icy cold mountains of China to see if she could find Abu Nazir.

Up until the time she met us she hadn't had much success in her quest because, when she did meet Abu Nazir, he cast a freezing spell on her, changed her into an ivory statuette and that would have been the end of her if I hadn't bought her as a Christmas present for my mum.

She was about halfway through the first bit of her story about the bandits when she stopped and said she'd tell us the rest some other time.

We all groaned, because it was interesting and asked why she'd stopped.

She fluttered her fan and her eyes twinkled.

'I am stopping,' she said, 'because the tide has turned and we are now sailing out to sea with no one at the tiller.'

'Glory Moses and boot laces!' yelled Old Man Noah, and rushed to the tiller. Fortunately Teddy got there first or we'd have landed straight back on that sandbank.

I went down below to my cabin again and climbed up into my bunk. It was still warm from all the bodies that had been sitting on it earlier that evening. I put my hands behind my head and gazed up at the hurricane lamp. It was throwing weird shadows all over the walls and the ceiling and I blinked, because in one corner there was a dark black shape which looked for all the world like a tall, thin, bony figure crouching over a crystal ball, watching me.

But then the ark rocked and the lamp swung about a bit and the shadows were broken up and just looked like ordinary shapes again. I blew out the lamp and snuggled down to sleep.

Shadow's Diary – Interruption 2

Once Kipper settled down to sleep the tall, slender, handsome young apprentice wizard straightened himself up from his cramped position over the crystal ball, rubbed his eyes and groaned.

It's no fun at all being assistant to a wicked magician. I daresay you think you'll learn lots of lovely magic spells so as to give people cramps and make 'em jump about yelling 'Oh, oh, oh!' But that's not my experience.

And I should know because I am that tall, slender, handsome young apprentice wizard and my name is Shadow and I have to spend most of my time staring into that crystal watching the respectable goings-on of the yukkiest collection of 'goodies' I've seen in my life.

I was bored out of my unpleasant little mind.

The only time I managed to have a bit of a gloat was when the mainsail came whizzing down and nearly hit Old Man Noah on the head but it wasn't much of a gloat because he didn't get hurt and what's the use of that! When people fall over I like 'em to break an arm or a leg, or, at the very least, get purple lumps on their heads and clutch at 'em and yell and prance about. There's no entertainment value in it otherwise, is there?

'Greetings, dear Shadow,' said a voice from the door. I swivelled my aching neck and saw my master Abu Nazir

looking in at me and smiling coldly. I hadn't heard a sound as he came up the stairs. I never do. He moves like a great cat.

'And how are all my enemies today, Shadow?' he asked. 'Still plotting against me?'

'Oh yes, dear master,' I assured him. 'Lots and lots of lovely plots. But then you have enemies the way other people have mice.'

'Naturally,' he said calmly. 'I am supposed to be a wicked magician and a wicked magician's success can only be calculated by the number of enemies he manages to acquire after all. Now, what of my principal enemy, the Lady Precious Pearl? She is still locked in that binding spell I put on her a few years ago?'

'No,' I said.

'No?' His eyes flickered and went cold.

I rubbed my hands together with glee. It really is lovely to have some bad news to tell someone, isn't it?

'No,' I said happily. 'She's escaped. Flown the coop.'

Abu Nazir stroked his pointed beard pensively.

'This is bad news for me,' he said softly.

'Yes, terrible isn't it!' I cried.

He nodded.

'It is very bad news,' he said delicately. 'So, dear Shadow, why are you smiling so happily?'

I choked.

'Me? I'm not smiling,' I gurgled. 'I was – er – grimacing. I've had an uncontrollable grimace for years. Had doctors for it and everything.'

My master frowned very slightly. 'Control your grimaces in future,' he said grimly. 'How did she escape from the spell?'

'A small boy with large ears bought her as a Christmas present for his mother and then a toy soldier kissed her and within a very short time she was stepping out very lively.'

Abu Nazir's face showed no sign of the rage and fury I'd hoped to see. It was almost impassive. 'Where is she now?'

'Fast asleep aboard a small wooden ark on the other side of the Midnight Mountains.'

'So she is coming into our world again, is she?' he said quietly. 'Watch her, Shadow. Watch her night and day and don't fail to warn me of any move that she makes. Of all my enemies she is potentially the most dangerous, for she is the seventh daughter of a seventh daughter and great, great granddaughter of Allah U Dhinn.'

'Seventh daughter of a seventh daughter, eh?' I said, as if I didn't already know.

'In the higher mathematics of magic there is something peculiarly potent about seventh daughters,' he nodded. 'And even more so when raised to the power of the square of seven. They elude the nets, they evade the traps, they escape from enchantments. Watch her, Shadow. I have not forgotten my experience with Aladdin.'

'Didn't get on with him, did you?' I said.

Abu Nazir shook his head and looked at me steadily. 'No,' he said. 'He stole the magic lamp from me in the darkness of a cave. It was then that I decided that never again would I choose as an assistant, a double-jointed, double-crossing, wily Oriental. Instead I decided to look round for the most stupid, short-sighted, congenital imbecile I could find. I found you.'

'Thanks very much,' I said sulkily.

He nodded and went out of the room, leaving me with that infernal crystal and the prospect of staring into it twenty-four hours a day. Yet I dare not think of offending him.

Abu Nazir held the magic lamp of power and as long as he had it I was his slave, his worm, his Shadow, and I dared not say a word, no matter how much he insulted me. I knew only too well that he had only to rub that lamp and he could release a genie so powerful it would rip, and bite and tear me to pieces. I didn't fancy that fate.

3 The Voyage Through the Midnight Mountains

I was up bright and early on the first full day of the voyage. It was cool on deck. Not cold exactly but the wind was certainly fresh and I felt it running its fingers through my hair and snatching at my pyjama jacket as I stood in the bows of the ark and surveyed the world at large.

The Midnight Mountains were on the port side and seemed to be coming closer and closer. They looked rather unfriendly now that I was able to look at them in more detail but, friendly or unfriendly, I still wanted to know what was on the other side of them. What lands, what strange seas peopled with wizards and monsters, hippogriffs and mermaids.

I looked back astern and saw the green hump of an island sticking up from the sea in our wake. It had four tall trees and the battlements of a fortress peeping up over the edge of the skyline. My island! All that was left of Mum's tatty old carpet. My world!

I looked around and saw, here and there, the isolated lumps of other islands scattered all over the seascape but they belonged to someone else and I couldn't see any of the details.

I turned my attention back to that range of coal black

mountains looming off the port bow. They seemed ever so big and pointed and jagged and they shone like black glass.

There was a fluttering of wings and the little green dragon perched itself on the rail beside me.

'Greetings, honourable Kipper,' it said. 'Man who rises early on cold day catches influenza. That's a Chinese proverb. Chinese very clever people. Manufacture proverbs by the hatful.'

Teddy Bear came lumbering up the forrard hatchway and rolled towards us with the motion of the ship.

'Hi, Ted,' I said cheerily. 'Seen Benjie anywhere?'

He regarded me from underneath his bushy eyebrows. 'Benjie is sitting on the steps leading up to the after deck,' he said. 'He is sitting with his head in his hands looking sad, sentimental and generally droopy.'

'Seasick?' I enquired.

Teddy shook his head. 'He is in love,' he explained. 'The – er – tender passion. Makes otherwise sensible

people look as if they've just swallowed a bag of quick-setting concrete. The result is that he is no fit company for man or bear, and, given the slightest encouragement, will start writing poetry.'

I decided to go in search of the love-struck soldier and I found him, just as Teddy had said, sitting on the steps leading up to the wheelhouse, but he wasn't sitting with his head clasped in his hands. He was industriously scribbling on a notepad propped on his knee with a stub of pencil he kept tucked in his busby.

I sneaked up on him and hid behind the mast.

'Dear Lady Precious Pearl,

I think you are a wondrous girl,' he chanted, testing the words.

'You crossed my path just like a comet.'

Here he paused and scratched his head. Old Man Noah trotted busily across the deck on some industrious Captain-type business of his own and Benjie hailed him.

'Noah!' he said. 'What rhymes wiv comet?'

'Vomit,' said Old Man Noah, and vanished.

'Great 'elp that is,' muttered Benjie.

I stepped out from my hiding place. 'Hallo, hallo, HALLO!' I bellowed. 'What's up, Benjie?'

He nearly jumped out of his scarlet jacket.

'Don't do that,' he grumbled. 'Creeping up on me . . .'

I squashed myself down beside him, and wriggled.

'Teddy tells me that you've fallen in love,' I said loud enough for the entire ship to hear and anyone in a passing island if they happened to be listening. 'Well I never. Fancy that. Blow me up, down and sideways. Who'd've thought it!'

Benjie rubbed his stubby little nose.

'Look 'ere,' he said plaintively. 'I will not have you tramping across me passion in your number nines.'

'But what's it feel like?' I persisted. 'I can't imagine it myself. Go on Benjie, tell Kipper.'

He shrugged.

'Feels a bit like stepping nonchalantly down a lift shaft,' he said. 'I didn't want it to 'appen, now did I? It just 'appened. Like catching measles, and now I'm stuck wiv it. I dream about her at night. I see her looking down at me from the walls of me cabin. I even saw her looking up at me from a plateful of cornflakes at breakfast this morning. So, I ate her.'

'But girls are so *useless*,' I pointed out reasonably.

'That's what I used to think,' said Benjie, and sighed. 'But now I can't get her out of my mind, not nohow.

She's so far above me, d'you see. She's so lovely, and pure, and – and – and . . .'

'Blimey,' I said. 'You have got it bad.'

'I'm only a toy soldier, you see, and she is so far above me that I could never 'ope to aspire, could I?'

But I'd had enough. I stood up.

'If you are going into your humble and modest routine, I'm off,' I announced. 'Time I had breakfast too. Mrs Noah is cooking bangers and mash, shlurp, shlurp.'

I left him to it and went and wheedled Mrs Noah into giving me an enormous helping.

Mrs Noah is Old Man Noah's wife, of course, and she does all the cooking aboard the ark. She is a very large lady, and we are all afraid of her because when she raises her voice it cuts your eardrums into strips. How, why or when Old Man Noah married her is a mystery because she makes three of him. She has a red face, dark eyes and she always wears a chef's hat and a flowered apron.

'Get along with you, Kipper,' she said, and put another dollop of mash on my plate. 'You'll bust if you eat all that.'

'No I won't,' I assured her.

'Well, if you do, I'm not going to clear up the mess,' she said and shook a finger like a sausage at me. 'Off wiv yer and don't get hiccups.'

I was enjoying this voyage in the ark. During the times we are at sea nothing much seems to happen and gradually a routine develops and you find yourself doing the same things every day, yet it's never dull or boring.

I always found myself sitting up on the deckhouse around mid-morning, with Teddy on one side and Benjie on the other, and we'd sit and watch the sea and the sky and we didn't bother to talk very much but it was cosy and friendly and that's what I like. Every now and again we'd hear Old Man Noah fall down a hatchway or trip over a ladder. Sometimes the little green dragon would come and perch on my shoulder and sometimes he'd stay with his mistress.

Every morning I stood by the deckrail and watched the mountains coming closer and closer.

'Hard a starboard,' cried the voice of the helmsman and Old Man Noah swung the tiller with great efficiency.

'That's port!' bellowed the helmsman.

'Oh bother!' said Noah.

Benjie strolled across the deck and took the tiller bar away from Noah. I walked across and joined him.

The bows of the ark were moving in a half circle and the ship seemed to be aiming straight for the black cliffs but, just as I was holding my breath and expecting to hear the crunching, grinding sound as we crashed into the rocks, I saw a narrow channel opening out with hardly room on either side for the ark to get through.

I put my hand out and actually touched the smooth rock wall on my side of the ark.

Benjie rubbed his nose and swung the tiller skilfully this way and that and we dodged in and out of the racing, swirling currents until the gorge widened into a dark river.

'Phew!' he said and pushed his busby back on his forehead as he relaxed.

'Tricky, that bit of the river,' he said. 'The currents come at you from all sides and the foam hides the rocks that sit there just below the surface waiting to bite the bottom out of any ship that's passing.'

Then he looked at me and grunted. 'Got your wish at last, haven't you, Kipper? I hope you don't regret it.'

'Why should I?'

Benjie's fingers tapped the edge of the tiller nervously.

'It's dangerous out there,' he said. 'Once you get beyond the Midnight Mountains anything can happen and it often does. Still, that's you all over isn't it, Kipper? Little trips to the enchanted forest aren't enough for you now, are they? You're beginning to demand real adventures and your demands are threatening to exceed our capacities. There's a limit to what me, and Teddy and Old Man Noah can do, yer know. Once we're out the other side and on the way to ancient Cathay, we're in a world where wicked magicians and various other assorted bogies can come popping up at any moment, and none of 'em are funny, I promise you, Kipper. None of 'em.'

His voice was very serious. I peered at him in the half dark, and my silly, sentimental old Benjie seemed different somehow. I suppose I'd always taken him and

Teddy and Old Man Noah for granted and I began to realize that there was a lot about them that I didn't know at all.

Teddy clumped up out of the darkness and lit his pipe.

'Benjie?' he said in his deepest growliest voice. 'What's up?'

'Nothing,' said Benjie casually.

'Oh yes there is,' said Teddy persistently, and he jabbed Benjie in the midriff with the stem of his pipe. 'First you were in love, and that caused you to mope all round the seascape heaving sighs and pulling funny faces, and vanishing out of sight every time Lady Precious Pearl took a stroll on deck.'

'No, I didn't,' said Benjie, sounding more like his old self.

'Oh yes you did,' said Teddy. 'Your ears went bright pink and you disappeared so fast your shadow was wandering round the ship for three hours trying to find you.'

Benjie opened his mouth to argue, thought better of it and shut it again.

'And now,' said Teddy, 'you're worried about something else. You can't fool me, y'know. I know you too well.'

I stood by the deckrail and watched the black gorges slipping by and I opened up my inquisitive big ears to listen to what they were saying because I'd never heard Teddy and Benjie talking together in quite this sort of way. Not since the time when I had mumps.

Benjie lowered his voice, but what he was saying still reached me because the night was very still, and I think the mountains round us magnified sound a little bit.

'I'm worried about Kipper,' Benjie said. 'I'm worried

about Abu Nazir. I'm worried about going beyond the Midnight Mountains and I'm worried about this here quest. I'm one big aching ball of worry, all over.'

'Humph,' said Teddy.

It was a comforting sort of 'Humph'. There's more solid comfort in one of old Ted's grunts than in any amount of conversation from anyone else.

'This whole quest,' Benjie went on, forgetting that I was only a few yards away looking up at the moon. 'It's dangerous, and it's our job to keep our bossy boots out of trouble. Not lead him into it. I don't know if I'm doin' the right thing in letting him come on this journey. I'm only a toy soldier and there's things I can't protect him against, nor you. Abu Nazir may well turn out to be one of 'em.'

Teddy blew a smoke ring, 'Yup,' he nodded, 'and ordinarily I'd agree with you Benjie, but there's one thing you're overlooking, my lad.'

'And what's that?'

'It isn't up to you, all the time, nor me, nor Old Man Noah. Lurking in the background of this quest there are the *Big Ones*.'

'Such as?'

'The golden dragon, for starters. I'd have advised turning back a long time ago if I hadn't realized the Big Ones were concerned in this. As it is I doubt if we can draw back. We go on with the quest because we *must*. It's what's intended for us and that, Benjie, includes our little bossy boots.'

The river was widening up into a curving bay and on one side of it I could see the outlines of a vast, deep forest.

I heard a light footstep near me and smelled a whiff of perfume, and when I turned my head I saw that Lady

Precious Pearl had come up on deck and quietly joined Benjie at the rail.

They both looked up at the moon and I saw a witch on a broomstick riding across it, just for a moment. I clomped across to join them.

'What's that forest?' I asked.

'Carbonek,' grunted Benjie. 'We'd better go below in a minute because it isn't healthy to be out in the open too near to Carbonek. It's haunted forest for the most part, and what haunts it ain't nice.'

'Why?' I asked.

Before Benjie had time to answer me the question was answered for him.

Thousands of bats came up from the forest. They fluttered out of the darkness to sit on the masts and the rigging of the ark. And there they perched, staring down at us with malevolent green eyes.

A cold, damp, clammy wind came with them and it swirled across the deck and we all shivered. I clutched Benjie's hand and squeezed it, just in case he was frightened.

Benjie looked down at me and his leathery, cheeky face was white and drawn. 'We're beyond the Midnight Mountains now, Kipper m'lad.'

The wind brought the stench of something rotting and decayed and my spirits sank down into my boots. All the courage oozed out of me. I felt very small, very alone and very defenceless.

'I d-didn't know it would be like this,' I muttered. 'I'm a bit frightened, Benjie. Only a bit,' I added, 'but it's rather a large bit.'

The bats flapped their leathery wings and their eyes glittered down at us.

'Excuse me one moment,' piped a clear little voice.

The tiny green dragon, all eight inches of him, strutted out on to the centre of the well deck, all alone. He paused, glanced round casually, gave a polite little cough to clear his throat and then puffed out a streak of flame. The bats squealed in horror and rose and flew away, a dark cloud of evil that slithered across the sky and then sank down into the forest.

'They will not bother us again,' said the little green dragon.

A warm wind flowed across the deck and we all began to feel better immediately.

'Told you the *Big Ones* were involved in this quest,' said Teddy to Benjie out of the side of his mouth. 'Small though he is, that little green dragon is one of the Big Ones really.'

Benjie scratched his nose. He always scratches his nose when he's thinking. 'Tell you what,' he said slowly. 'We're gonna need some help. There's no one here who is quite up to tackling Abu Nazir direct. The little green dragon wasn't strong enough to prevent Precious Pearl being frozen into an ivory statuette. We've also gotta find out where the magician hides the magic lamp.'

'We could tie him up and put lighted matches between his toes,' I suggested eagerly. 'I read about that in a book at school.'

'Bloodthirsty ha'porth,' grinned Benjie. 'You and your books.'

'I don't think that Abu Nazir is the sort of magician to take kindly to such treatment,' said Teddy.

'Definitely *not*,' murmured Old Man Noah who had been listening attentively. 'And it's no use asking *me* to tie him up because my knots always come undone. My bowlines turn out to be all line and no bow and my sheepshanks have never worried a sheep or a shank.'

Lady Precious Pearl fluttered her fan. 'What do you suggest we do then?'

Benjie pointed ahead. We all turned and looked out across the sea. The ark was just rounding the point of the long strip of land called Carbonek and as it made its way round the outer edges of it I saw a stretch of desolate wilderness that reached right across an even bigger bay. But, far away, almost as if it was surrounded by haunted Carbonek on one side and the desolate wilderness on the other, I saw a tall shining white castle with tower after tower all over it like candles on a birthday cake.

'Camelot,' said Benjie quietly.

'*Camelot!*' I gurgled.

'Many-towered Camelot where the knights of King Arthur once sat at the Round Table and fought evil in their own fashion. The knights have gone now, all except one. Sir Roland de Hainault still waits there for one last quest and this may well be it. At all events I need his advice so we're going to anchor offshore, march across the wilderness and have a chat with him. He's an old friend of mine. A soldier like me, y'see. It'll be nice ter see him again. Good bloke, Sir Roland. You'll like him.'

I put my hands on my hips and glared at my surprising toy soldier. 'I didn't know you knew a knight of King Arthur,' I said indignantly. 'You never told *me*.'

'I don't tell you everything, Kipper,' said Benjie, and rubbed my hair. 'No more does Ted.'

Teddy Bear grunted. 'Of course not,' he said. 'We're the guards. It'll be pleasant to renew an old acquaintance and if Sir Roland can help us I'm sure he will. He's like that. Filled to the brim with the Arthurian vice of gratuitous interference. So, if there's a damsel to be rescued or a wicked magician to kill, Sir Roland is unquestionably our man.'

'Set course for Camelot,' Benjie said to Old Man Noah, 'and, in the meantime, below decks, Kipper, and get some sleep 'cos we've a long walk tomorrow.'

I went. But, just before I clumped off down the

hatchway to my cabin I glanced back at the moon and I caught my breath.

'*Look*!' I said, and pointed up at the sky.

The moon was full and yet there was a cloud wrack round it and for one brief moment the moon looked like a crystal ball with an eye glowering down at all of us and the clouds were hunched into the shape of a thin, bony figure crouched over a crystal and watching us – watching us all.

Then the cloud dissolved and the sky was clear and the moon was just a moon again.

I went down to my cabin but all night I felt as though I was being watched. It was a most unpleasant feeling. I had bad dreams that night.

Shadow's Diary – Interruption 3

'Well,' said Abu Nazir as I came rushing in with the latest news.

'Master,' I said. 'They are all of 'em leaving the ark and they are tramping across the wilderness to see a knight at Camelot Castle. I thought you'd like to know.'

'A knight?' he said. 'One of King Arthur's knights?'

'Yes,' I replied promptly. 'Name of Sir Roland.'

He brooded quietly.

'Someone is being very clever, aren't they, Shadow? You'd better leave at once and forestall them.'

'I'd never get there in time,' I protested. 'It's a long way to Camelot from here.'

'You can use one of my flying carpets,' he said.

'Oh, thank you, thank you, dear kind master,' I cried, grovelling suitably. Being given a magic carpet to fly about on was really going up in the world because he didn't usually let me get near anything as genuinely magic as that.

'Oh shut up,' he said wearily.

He turned and left the room and went down the stairs, his robes blowing out behind him. I scrambled down after him as fast as I could but I was puffing and gasping by the time we reached his throne room because he moved very fast. It was like trying to keep up with the wind.

He pointed to a small carpet in the darkest corner of the room.

'That one will do,' he said. 'Fly to Camelot and see to it that Lady Precious Pearl does not reach Sir Roland. And don't make your usual mess of it.'

I swallowed the insult as best I could.

'How does it work?' I said. 'The carpet I mean. What do I say to make it fly to Camelot? Are there any magic words or runic spells?'

'No,' he said, to my disappointment. 'Just tell it what you want it to do and where you want it to go. Every thread is impregnated with spells.'

'Right,' I said. 'Well, here goes.'

I cleared my throat and in a loud, clear, ringing voice I said, 'Carpet! Rise up in the air.'

It did.

It shot straight up in the air with me standing in the middle of it and the top of my head hit the ceiling with a sickening thump.

'Wow!' I shrieked. 'Come down again you blithering idiot.'

The carpet promptly tipped me off and I crashed to the floor while that confounded rug remained happily glued to the ceiling.

My master, Abu Nazir, sat on his throne and I noticed his fingers were tapping gently.

'It is a rather literal carpet,' he observed. 'It naturally chose the only blithering idiot in the room.'

'Carpet,' I said grimly, 'come down at once.'

It came – straight down on my head flattening me to the floor. I crawled out spitting wool and dust. It hadn't been cleaned in years.

Abu Nazir laced his long, slender fingers together and looked at me icily.

'Are you ever going?' he enquired.

'Yes, master. At once, master,' I gurgled.

I stood on the carpet again and this time I thought very carefully before I issued any instructions. I could see I was going to have difficulties. A mentally defective carpet isn't as easy to control as I'd imagined.

'Carpet,' I said. 'We – that is to say you and I together – are going to Camelot Castle. Got that?'

It quivered under my feet. I could see it was anxious to please.

'Not yet,' I said sternly. It subsided.

'Now, in order to get there with maximum ease and dignity we have, first of all, to get out of this throne room. Therefore, rise gently in the air, turn and then go out of those eastern windows over there.'

The carpet rose two yards in the air as requested and swivelled itself towards the eastern windows as I had directed, and then, gathering speed perceptibly, it shot towards them like a bullet.

'Not the one that's still closed!' I yelled.

But it was too late. We crashed through the glass and for the rest of the journey I was picking splinters out of the most delicate places. And what was worse I was almost sure I heard my master, Abu Nazir, laughing to himself as I left the palace with a window frame draped round my neck.

Ooooh, I hated him. But I had to obey him. I couldn't wait to get my thieving hands on that magic lamp!

4 Trapped

We started out fairly early on our trek to Camelot Castle because Benjie said it was a long walk across the desolate wilderness.

I'm not exactly pleased with myself when I look back on what happened for I certainly didn't show up in the brightest and best of lights.

The ark reached the coastline in the very early hours of the morning and Old Man Noah dropped the anchor just a few yards from a pebbly beach. Unfortunately he forgot to let go of it when he dropped it, so we all heard a loud yell, followed by an ominous splash, and we had to throw him a lifebelt.

We pulled him aboard and he sat there streaming with water and being made a great fuss of by his animals, but his blue eyes were as mild and uncomplaining as ever as he blinked round at us all.

'Some people never learn, do they?' he said cheerfully. 'D'you know, I sank three times before I remembered I could swim.'

Little catastrophes like that are always happening to Old Man Noah but I've never heard him complain about it. He just gets up and carries on as if it hadn't happened at all. Which makes my behaviour all the worse I suppose.

We started out very briskly and I was full of the joys of living, and trotted along with Benjie and Teddy, Noah and Lady Precious Pearl, eager and ready to walk to Camelot and slap one of King Arthur's knights on the back, but the walk was a lot longer than I'd anticipated.

We tramped for miles and miles and my legs began to ache and my stomach felt emptier and emptier. I don't like being hungry. Nor do I like my legs aching. So I started to whine at everybody, and blame them, and ask stupid questions like 'How far is it now?' and 'I thought you knew the way?' and 'Haven't we got anything to eat?' I could hear myself doing it yet I couldn't stop it.

The desolate wilderness isn't a very interesting place to walk across at any time. It is flat and featureless and there's nothing to see but long stretches of yellow mud punctuated by vivid green rushes, a few small, stunted trees, and a succession of very smelly bogs which breed flies and gnats and midges, which rise up in clouds and bite and sting and buzz round your head and won't go away.

And then, about halfway across, a mist rose up and obscured the castle and it was obvious to me that even Benjie didn't really know whether we were going in the right direction or walking round and round in endless circles.

I began to nag at him in that horrible whiny voice, although I was the one who was always egging him on to let me have an adventure. No one else complained. Old Man Noah hummed a little song to himself but that began to get on my nerves after a while because it had one of those silly tiddley om pom pom tunes that goes on forever and never gets anywhere.

Lady Precious Pearl followed Benjie without ever seeming to get tired and she certainly didn't complain and I ought to have been ashamed to let a mere girl beat me. But, by the time we finally reached the outer walls of Camelot, I hated everyone, especially cheerful old men who hummed and girls who plodded on putting one foot in front of the other without moaning about everything.

The mist lifted and we saw a signpost, and the signpost clearly pointed down the same path, so Benjie *had* guided us correctly after all. I ought to have apologized. But I didn't.

We reached the outer wall of Camelot Castle about dinner time and I felt a bit better when I saw that we were at last in sight of food and shelter.

A tall hooded figure came hobbling towards us, and

bowed. He was obviously a hermit, or a pilgrim. He had a long white beard and leaned on a staff.

'Welcome to Camelot Castle,' he said. 'I am the ancient gateman. I will show you the way in.'

He swept his arm sideways and indicated a narrow path that led around the walls of the castle.

Benjie looked puzzled.

'That's not the way to the main entrance,' he said sharply.

I daresay Benjie was tired too. He always gets snappy when he's irritable.

'I know,' said the pilgrim and bowed again. 'This is a detour because the main entrance is under repair. The portcullis is jammed. They are still trying to extricate the last visitor. Follow me.'

Like idiots we all meekly followed him, although I did hear Teddy mumbling about his whiskers twitching.

Benjie turned on him.

'Teddy,' he said. 'Do me a favour, will you? Next time you have an 'aircut, have a shave.'

So Teddy shut up.

The pilgrim, or hermit, or whatever he was supposed to be, led us to a small side door in one of the towers and then into a long stone passageway, down some steps, along another draughty corridor and then stopped by an arched doorway set in the darkest bit of that draughty passage.

'Go through this Norman arch,' he said, 'and take the first turning on the left and *do* watch out for the Anglo Saxon OUCH, just beyond it. That will take you to the main hall, where, I'm sure, Sir Roland will welcome such distinguished visitors.'

He opened the door and we all trooped inside like tame

rabbits, and then the door was slammed behind us and we heard him cackling with laughter and cracking his knuckles with glee.

'Got you,' he said, through the doorway. 'You are trapped in a dark, dank, dismal dungeon and you will never get out. No one knows you're there, 'cept *me*. You'll die . . . slowly. First hunger, then thirst and then you'll go mad, mad, MAD! Oh what a lovely gloat I'm going to have. Farewell!'

We looked at each other, then at our surroundings. We were in a small dungeon with bars at the window and damp green slime running down the walls and cobwebs and spiders galore. A rat ran across the stone floor and yickered at us. It was too much for me. Just as I'd been looking forward to food, and shelter and meeting Sir Roland I was locked in a dungeon and there seemed no chance of getting out. So I threw a tantrum. I howled, and cried, and kicked the floor and blamed Benjie and Teddy and Old Man Noah, and when Lady Precious Pearl tried to cuddle me I flung off her hands and slapped out at her and left a red mark on her wrist.

The little green dragon fluttered from her shoulder and stood in front of me.

'Do not do that again, ever,' he said sternly. 'It is my task to protect my mistress from anyone who tries to harm her, and that, honourable Kipper, means you. Friends can hurt more than enemies sometimes.'

I burst into tears. No one loved me! Not even the little green dragon.

Shadow's Diary – Interruption 4

I have just done the dirty on Lady Precious Pearl and her friends and locked 'em all in a dank, dark and dismal dungeon. It took a bit of planning on my part, I can tell you, and it happened like this.

As I flew across the sky on that mentally defective flying carpet I thought long, hard and deep about that wretched Chinese dancing girl and her companions. They were, whichever way you looked at it, a pretty mixed-up bunch: a small boy, a Teddy Bear, a baldheaded old coot who fell over his feet every ten minutes and a Cockney toy soldier, to say nothing of a little green dragon. But, ill assorted though they appeared to be, they had one thing in common. They were all of 'em 'goodies' and I am a baddie and we baddies must always do our best to thwart, upset and torment goodies. The universe shall fall apart else! I decided I would have to do something really unpleasant to the lot of them.

We arrived over Camelot Castle within a few hours of leaving Abu Nazir's secret palace. I peeped over the edge of the carpet and surveyed the land below.

'In a minute or two,' I said to the carpet, 'I am going to ask you to land, see?'

The carpet curled one end of itself up into an S-shape and nodded.

'When I ask you to land,' I said carefully, 'you will not drop like a stone from beneath me, leaving me to follow as best I may. You will not land upside down in a prickly bush nor on top of a church steeple, or any of the more uncomfortable places your warped sense of humour may tempt you to find. Got that?' The carpet nodded again.

'Good,' I said briskly, and gave my hands a rub to show it I was pleased.

Below me I saw the muddy track that led towards Camelot Castle and I knew it was the one which the toy soldier and his friends would have to follow.

I saw a crossroads with a signpost, and a little further, almost under the wall of the castle, I saw a stretch of soft, vivid green grass.

I chuckled to myself. It was ideal.

'Carpet,' I said. 'You see that stretch of soft, vivid green grass down there? Well – that's where you land.'

The carpet dipped.

'Wait!' I shrieked. 'You descend very slowly and land me very gently without a bump on that stretch of soft, vivid green grass.'

The carpet banked and began a long, slow glide towards the stretch of soft, vivid green grass. It slithered to a fullstop.

'Thank you,' I said. 'Congratulations. You've done it right for once.'

I stepped off the carpet and went straight down under five feet of smelly, slimy green water. I came up, spluttering. I glared at the carpet. The carpet shrugged its pile at me and then flowed on to the nearby road. I squelched out of the bog and sat down by the walls of the castle.

'Why does it always happen to me?' I asked.

There was no answer. So, while my robes dried out and I donned a suitable disguise I conjured up a white mist that covered the wilderness.

That little trick slowed Benjie and his companions down quite a lot and I was able to reach the castle, put on my hermit disguise, and hobble out to meet them.

I locked them all in that dank, dark and dismal dungeon and rushed back to the carpet so as to return to the palace as fast as I could, and watch them as they slowly starved to death in the cells of Camelot Castle, a mere stone's throw away from Sir Roland.

I intended to have a prolonged gloat.

5 Rescue

I'd behaved very badly and I knew it. I recovered more or less, and sat up and began to take a bit of notice although I still felt snuffly and I had a headache. I went and sat on Teddy's lap for comfort.

'I want to get out of here, Teddy,' I said.

'So do we all,' he growled. 'But console yourself, Kipper. This is an adventure.'

'No it isn't,' I sniffed. 'It's *horrid*.'

'Adventures,' said Teddy Bear solemnly, 'usually are horrid. For the people looking on at them or reading about them, they may be great fun, but for the people in 'em they are invariably uncomfortable.'

'There must be some way out of this dungeon,' I said. 'Think of a plan, someone.'

Benjie came stomping across the dungeon, scratching his nose as usual. 'I've thought of 'undreds of plans,' he confessed. 'Trouble is, none of 'em are the right sort of plan. The sort that works.'

It was at that precise moment that I heard a strange weird noise from somewhere quite nearby. We all heard it and we stopped talking and listened intently. I don't know how to describe it. It was a thin, tinkly, peculiar noise that wobbled about all over the place as if it couldn't find its feet.

'Can you hear it too?' I asked Benjie.

The toy soldier nodded and wiggled his ears about. 'Yerse!' he said tersely. 'Sounds like a bilious attack looking for a stomach to happen in.'

'I expect it's the plumbing,' said Old Man Noah. 'You're bound to get a few gurgles in a place so old-fashioned the bathroom goes right round the outside.'

I was staring at the opposite wall, trying to fix the direction of the sound, when the solid bricks went all misty and a hand, followed by an arm, followed by a thin wavery body actually floated through the brickwork

of the dungeon and stood smiling at us. Needless to say, there was instant panic. Lady Precious Pearl squeaked. Benjie jumped as if he'd been stung. The little green dragon loosed off a tongue of flame but is simply went straight through the visitor without disturbing him in the least. He stood there and continued smiling pleasantly at us.

Old Man Noah tried diving up under his own robe to hide, but it wasn't a conspicuous success, and I hid behind Teddy Bear.

Our visitor was clearly a ghost. I'd never seen a spook before and I hadn't the faintest idea what to do, so I stayed plonked firmly behind Teddy's broad back.

'Wh – wh – who are you?' said Benjie nervously.

The wivery, wavery creature beamed ethereally. 'I'm a spook,' he said. 'I've been a spook for years. I go with the castle. Every properly equipped castle has a resident spook. I say,' he added eagerly, 'that was a really first-class panic just now. Were you really frightened? So encouraging because I've always been rather a failure at haunting you know. I do all the right things. I rattle chains and gibber at people. I gibber most frightfully, but I had to give it up in the end. *Do* ask me why.'

'Why?' asked Benjie.

'I was frightened of humans,' tittered the spook. 'Ridiculous, isn't it. So I settled down here to practise my music. I'm a flautist.'

'A what?' said Old Man Noah.

'A flautist. One who plays a flaut,' said the spook. 'I am the ghost of the second flautist in the minstrel gallery quartet but I fell out of the gallery and that put an end to an otherwise talented career.'

I noticed that he was dressed in a vaguely medieval

costume, and he carried a long, tubular instrument in his hands.

'Was that your music we heard just now?' asked Teddy.

'Yes,' he simpered. 'Did you like it?'

'No,' said Teddy.

The spook looked slightly crestfallen. 'Nobody does,' he sniffed sadly. 'And I practise so hard too. An artist does like to be appreciated. Communication is of the essence. Personally I believe someone pushed me out of that gallery because there's a lot of jealousy among musicians you know. Oh dear, no one ever wants to hear me play. Not even Sir Roland. He says it gives him indigestion.'

Benjie leapt forward, his face alight with interest.

'Do you know Sir Roland?' he asked eagerly.

'Known him for years, duckie,' said the spook. 'He lets me practise in the remoter parts of the castle.'

'We're *saved*,' yelled Benjie. 'Spooky – I like your music.'

Old Man Noah tugged his white hair worriedly. 'You just said it sounded like a bilious attack looking for a stomach to happen in,' he pointed out.

'Nothing sets me feet tapping faster than the sound of a first-class bilious attack,' said Benjie promptly.

The spook looked positively dazzled by this praise.

'At last,' he said. 'A discerning critic! I will now play my latest composition, entitled . . .'

But Benjie cut in quickly before he could start.

'Do me a favour, Spooky,' he said.

'For my public, anything!'

'Waft yourself back through those solid walls again, go and find Sir Roland and tell him that Corporal Benjie and a group of passionate music lovers are locked in his dungeon and will he please come and let 'em out.'

'Done,' said the spook, and melted away through the walls.

'We're *saved*!' yelled Benjie, and he began to waltz Lady Precious Pearl all over the dungeon, while the rest of us thumped each other on the back and chortled merrily.

About ten minutes later we heard firm footsteps marching along the passage, a key was inserted in the lock, bolts were dragged aside and the door of our dungeon burst open and there, standing in the doorway, was Sir Roland de Hainault looking every inch a knight of King Arthur.

He was tall with very broad shoulders, and he had golden hair that glittered and flashed, and his eyes were warm and twinkly and a deep cornflower blue.

'Sir Benjie!' he cried. 'My little toy soldier! How wondrous to see you again. Introduce me to your friends and tell me how came you into this most parlous plight.'

And he swept into the room and smiled round at one and all.

Benjie saluted, and pulled Lady Precious Pearl into clear view. 'This is the Lady Precious Pearl,' he said, 'a damsel in distress whom it is hoped you may be able to help.'

Sir Roland bent and kissed her hand and her eyelids went all fluttery as she looked up at him. 'Welcome, my lady,' he said, 'and if there is any small deed of arms I can undertake on your behalf you have only to command me.'

He kissed her hand again.

After all the introductions, Sir Roland led us upstairs to the great hall where a huge banquet was served and I ate everything in sight, including *three* helpings of seed cake.

Shadow's Diary – Interruption 5

There's no doubt about it, I am not lucky. I've never been lucky. And it's not fair! I locked those horrible goodies up in a dank, dark, dismal dungeon, and I therefore had every right to expect that my nasty little plan would work. I wanted to watch 'em suffer too. So, as soon as I'd slammed the door and bolted it, I rushed down the corridors of Camelot Castle, called the flying carpet to heel and said to it, 'Go back to the crystal room on the left-hand side of Abu Nazir's palace by the fastest possible route.'

It went. It went by the fastest possible route too. And the fastest possible route led through three thick hedges covered in sharp thorns, a pig-sty and a farmhouse with very low beams.

I was hardly in a fit state to enjoy a gloat by the time we sailed in through the window of the crystal room. Nonetheless, determined to miss as little as possible of their sufferings, I rushed to the crystal and focused it on the dungeon at Camelot and I was just in time to see Benjie and the little green dragon trying out one of the plans that didn't work.

There were burn marks all round the door where the dragon had been trying to make an impression on the lock, but the whole door was made of iron and he hadn't enough puff to make any real headway.

Then Benjie stuffed the gunpowder from his bullets in the

lock and the dragon puffed out a streak of flame and there was a loud bang and Benjie came down the stairs to the dungeon on his head.

I giggled. I rubbed my hands together in an ecstasy of malicious glee. I was beginning to enjoy myself. And then my whole malevolent plan was undone by a passing ghost who wasn't even a good musician. I could have cried. I stamped my foot and howled with rage and frustration.

'So,' said a quiet voice beside me, 'you had them all locked up in a dank, dark, dismal dungeon did you, dear Shadow?'

And there was Abu Nazir himself, looking over my shoulder into the crystal.

What could I say? Not a rag of an excuse could I offer.

'It's not my fault, master,' I howled. 'I left 'em all in a dank, dark, dismal dungeon and it was a lovely bit of villainy and now it's all undone again.'

We both watched silently as the dungeon door opened and Sir Roland greeted Benjie like a long lost brother and kissed Lady Precious Pearl's hand, the way knights always do, and then we saw him lead them out of the dungeon and up to the great hall. It made me sick.

Abu Nazir looked at me for a long, long time. He didn't say a word. Then he pointed his finger up towards the ceiling and muttered a short spell. A huge brick came away from the mortar and landed on top of my head. I sagged.

'Shadow,' he said, very quietly. 'Shall I tell you something?'

'What, dear master?' I groaned.

'I don't like you,' he said.

And the floor opened and I fell with a howl down five storeys and wound up in the cellar.

My master peered down at me through the opening.

'I never have,' he added, and went away.

6 The Banquet at Camelot Castle

The great hall at Camelot was a very impressive place with massive walls and high arched columns and lots of shields and tapestries hung here and there, mainly to keep out draughts. Flaming torches in iron brackets flared smokily down on each side but the smoke went curling up through a hole in the roof so the hall itself didn't get smothered in smog.

At the far end there was a long table on a raised platform and that was where we sat down and waited for the banquet to begin. I don't know what Mum would have thought because there was no tablecloth and no knives or forks.

Sir Roland clapped his hands and immediately dishes began to float through the air from the other end of the hall and the whole meal was served out to us by invisible servants.

I'd never been to a banquet where the food was served out by invisible hands and it's a bit uncanny to see plates skidding to a halt in front of you and double-pronged forks coming out of thin air as they stab a chunk of venison pie and dollop it on the plate in complete silence. But I didn't let it put me off my food.

I'm beginning to think that food plays a much more

important part in an adventure than it does in ordinary, everyday life. At home it turns up at regular intervals and Mum is always there to cook it, and be complained at, if she gives you Brussels sprouts when you don't like Brussels sprouts, but, in an adventure, you never know when your next meal is going to arrive, so when it does, you grab it and you eat it.

I can imagine the scene there'd be at home if poor old Mum tried to give me venison pie with the meat cooked to rags in a hot, red wine sauce, but at Camelot I ate everything that was offered and never once did I say, 'Ugh – what's that? I don't like it.'

While we ate, Sir Roland asked about our quest and Benjie and Precious Pearl brought him up to date on it and he stroked his chin and looked very thoughtful.

'I trust you have dined well, my lady,' he said in his courtly fashion to Precious Pearl when the meal at last ended.

She twinkled up at him and replied in an equally grave and polite voice, 'To one accustomed to the frugality of rice and noodles, your medieval banquet comes as quite a shock. By the time we had reached the eighth course I was not sure whether I was undertaking a course of physical exercise or indulging in a way of life.'

Sir Roland looked pleased. 'Always kept a good table,' he said.

He laughed down at her. She fluttered her eyelashes up at him. They were getting on fine together. You could see that a mile away.

We stretched our legs and wandered out to the battlements of the castle and Sir Roland began to talk quietly and seriously about ye goode olde days when the knights of the Round Table lived at Camelot. He told us how they slew bad knights and fought wickedness.

Listening to Sir Roland, it seemed to me that Sir Lancelot, and Sir Gawaine, and Sir Bedevere were always rushing about fighting people and when they ran out of people to fight they held tournaments and bashed each other. I didn't quite see the point of it myself, and neither did Benjie.

He was sitting next to me on the ramparts, with his behind jammed into one of those oblong openings in the battlements where archers used to fire arrows. He wriggled uncomfortably and waved his arms about and said, 'Speakin' fer meself, I leave the world alone and it wags on pretty well without me trying to alter it.'

Sir Roland smiled, and then his face went all remote and stern, and he sighed. 'If the gardener looks not to his garden, Sir Benjie,' he said slowly, 'weeds will soon choke the flowers and the vegetables in his plot. Where then is beauty and chivalry, or even plain potatoes for lowly folk to eat withal? Come,' he said, 'I will show you the armoury. You'd like to see that would you not, Sir Kipper?'

And he looked straight at me.

'Yes,' I said eagerly. 'Rather!'

He led us down a long flight of winding stone stairs, through an arched doorway to a gallery. At the end of this gallery there was another door made of stout oak and it was bolted and barred.

Sir Roland spoke a few words in a strange language and the bolts sprang back and the bars dropped away and the door opened without a squeak. He motioned us in ahead of him.

Here, in the very centre of the castle, there was a high

vaulted chamber. Sir Roland flicked his fingers and invisible hands rushed around lighting up the torches and by the orange, smoky light we saw that in this room there was gathered together every kind of weapon that ever there was; from the earliest flint tipped arrows to bronze spears, iron swords, battle axes, maces, lances and daggers.

'Behold,' said Sir Roland, 'here's an array of biffing equipment, eh? And each one is double edged.'

'What d'you mean?' I asked.

'Every weapon here can be used to defend truth, justice and freedom, but each one, in the hands of wicked men, can also be used to inflict tyranny, oppression and misery. And the grave danger is this, my friends, that in even the best, and most well-intentioned hands, the one can always become the other.'

'Quite so,' muttered Old Man Noah beside me.

'True, true. Ho yus, very true,' mumbled Benjie on the other side.

Teddy Bear didn't say anything. He simply stood with his paws clasped behind his back and looked round at the weapons with a very sceptical eye.

Sir Roland smiled sadly. Then he put his hands on my shoulders and stared at me as if he was making up his mind whether to say something or not. I don't like being looked at like that. It makes me uncomfortable. So I fidgeted about on one foot and went red.

'To use weapons wisely in order to defend the true, the good and the helpless,' he said at last, 'you must needs be bound by an oath under the High God, and to know the meaning of your promise to fight only in the defence of goodness against evil. To do that you must needs join an Order, as I have done, and learn to tell that which is wicked from that which is good. Perhaps evil is a disease and needs a cure, but wickedness is an action and must therefore be fought. You have to learn how to tell bad from good and right from wrong. Clever lies can be made to sound like very truth, Sir Kipper, and ruthless, selfish, ambitious men can use fair words to cloak their intentions. Why, there are those who can quote the Gospel of our Lord in order to appear righteous.'

'Wh-what Order do you belong to then?' I said nervously.

'To the Most Christian Order of the Knights of Arthur Pendragon,' he replied. 'And those who join us may well have to be prepared to – er – biff people. For the world cannot, alas, be left to wag on by itself as Sir Benjie there would like to believe. We are, when necessity drives, the sword of God, you see.'

Sir Roland fell silent and wouldn't say any more on the subject, but he left me feeling very upset and peculiar inside. I wandered away with Benjie and Teddy and Old Man Noah, leaving Lady Precious Pearl and the little green dragon with Sir Roland. We found ourselves outside in the outer bailey and I plumped myself down on the brickwork round a well and curled my hand round the windlass.

Benjie poked his face forward and stared at me.

'What's up, Kipper?' he asked anxiously.

'Nothing,' I said, and kicked my feet against the side of the well.

He felt my pulse and then told me to put my tongue out.

'Why've you gone all droopy?' he demanded. He was getting a bit of his own back.

'I'm not in love,' I said defensively. 'I'm not *that* daft.'

'Indigestion,' said Teddy. 'Distinct case of overdose of seed cake. Three helpings. I saw you. I shuddered inside. It's very tricky stuff, seed cake. My uncle Bruin ate some once and in a matter of hours he had flowers sprouting out all over his chest and weeds in areas I won't specify. We sprayed him with weedkiller, and mowed him once a week, but all to no avail. Mind you, my aunt Bruin said it was nice to have flowers in the house all the time but . . .'

'It wasn't seed cake,' I shouted. 'It's Sir Roland and all that knightly chivalry stuff. I'm beginning to feel noble and self sacrificing and I've never felt like that before. I don't want to be noble, and Christian and that guff.'

Teddy Bear laughed.

Old Man Noah waved his telescope in the air and pranced about, chuckling.

Benjie slapped his knee and gurgled like a gargoyle.

'D'you know what's the matter with you, Kipper?' he grinned. 'You're growing up.'

'I don't wanna grow up!' I howled furiously. 'I want to be the sort of boy I've always been. I understood myself perfectly then. I was going to dig up treasure, and when I'd got it, I was going to spend all of it on *me*! I was going to be a pirate and make all my teachers walk the plank. Especially old Wallopchops who teaches sums. What's the use of being a pirate and making all that effort, eh? Why make all the teachers walk the plank if I'm then supposed to dive in and save 'em. Fancy diving in and saving old Wallopchops. Waste of a good plank, that is.'

There was a fluttering of wings and the little green dragon landed on the handle of the windlass.

'Please to excuse interruption of conversation at most soul-searching moment,' he piped, 'but your presence is requested in the mirror room by Sir Roland, immediately.'

'Show us the way,' said Benjie, and stomped off after the little green dragon, followed by Old Man Noah and Teddy.

I slumped after them and Old Man Noah turned, beamed at me kindly out of his mild blue eyes, and patted me gently on the head.

'Don't worry,' he said. 'You've had an overdose of sanctity. Often happens, but it'll soon straighten itself out, my boy.'

'I *do* hope so,' I said. 'I feel all stretched and strained inside.'

He nodded.

'No one is going to ask you to become one of King Arthur's knights just yet,' he said gently. 'Come on, let's see what surprises await us in the mirror room, eh. You've never seen Merlin's mirror, have you? Quite an experience.'

'What's Merlin's mirror?' I asked.

'You'll find out,' said Old Man Noah, and led me into the castle again.

7 The Mirror of Merlin

I stalked into the mirror room, quivered with indignation because it seemed to me that everyone knew all about things that I didn't know at all. Benjie was an old friend of Sir Roland's. Teddy Bear was another old friend of Sir Roland's. Old Man Noah knew all about this mirror, and I didn't know anything about anything. I glared round the room, looking for this celebrated mirror.

Sir Roland was standing beside Lady Precious Pearl and Teddy, Noah and Benjie were gathered together in a group waiting for something to happen. The little green dragon came and perched itself on my shoulder and that mollified me but I still couldn't see anything that looked in the least like a mirror.

There was, against one wall of the room, an oval sheet of polished metal with scroll work and the outline of an old man with a long beard and a pointed hat around the edge of it, but that wasn't a mirror, nor anything like it so far as I was concerned. Mirrors are made of glass

'Behold,' said Sir Roland, 'the mirror of Merlin,' and waved his hand at the sheet of polished metal.

I glowered at it. If you stood very close to it you could just about see yourself in it but that was all. I sniffed.

'Many, many centuries ago,' said Sir Roland, 'the great

Mage, Merlinus Ambrosius, adviser to my Liege Lord King Arthur, caused this mirror to be wrought out of iron and bronze. And, when the metal was in molten state, he poured into it his own powers of seeing the past, and the future. When any man stands in front of the mirror he can, of course, see the simple reflection of himself, which is the present, but, given the permission of the guardian of the castle, he can, if he so wishes, look into the future or see far back into the past. Once, many centuries ago, I asked that I might behold my own future and my wish was granted, though Merlin warned me against it. I was young and impetuous in those days, and I insisted. Doubtless I hoped to see myself in battle, winning, against odds, some famous tournament, or maybe I hoped to see myself bringing honour and fame to the Round Table by slaying a monster, or rescuing a damsel. Who knows? I saw none of those things. I saw instead a face looking back at me from my own future. It was the face of a young woman and she had hair black as night and a skin the colour of amber and eyes that tilted sideways a little. I knew of no damsel or maiden who had such a cast of feature, but the mirror revealed her to me and Merlin said that she would beckon me out on my last quest and I must wait for her. For years I searched, but then I returned to Camelot, having failed ever to see her, and Merlin met me at the gate and told me that I must now wait in the castle for as long as need be. Time stands still in enchanted Camelot, but little did I know that centuries would pass before she came to this place. Yet she is here and she does indeed request of me that I should accompany her on one last and final quest, before I too go to Avalon.'

The knight paused. 'As guardian of Camelot and of the

mirror of Merlin I can consult the mirror and it will tell me precisely where the magician Abu Nazir hides the magic lamp of power. Nothing can be concealed from this mirror, my friends, for everything is either in the past, the present, or the future. Is it your wish that I should ask the mirror to reveal this secret?'

Benjie cleared his throat and nodded. 'Yus,' he said. 'S'matter of fact that was one of my reasons for coming here though I kept it tucked away under me busby.'

Everyone shuffled their feet and nodded, so Sir Roland turned towards the mirror and began to speak in that strange language again.

The mirror clouded over, for all the world as if someone had breathed on it. It went steamy and misty and colours began to chase each other over it. We all moved closer. It cleared. We all blinked in amazement.

It was as if there was now an oval-shaped hole in the wall and we were looking through it into a different part of the world altogether. I suppose we were.

There, in front of us, as clear, and so near it looked as if we could stretch through and touch it, there was a palace with towers and minarets and gardens, all enclosed within the high, circling ramparts of a mountain range that was even bigger than the Midnight Mountains.

'Kiangsu,' murmured Lady Precious Pearl. 'There is the peak of the White Lady of Chen Su, and over there the twin pinnacles of the Two Brothers, and there, that yellow streaked mountain is the Tiger's Eye. It will be easy to find the place now.'

'Watch,' said Sir Roland quietly. It was like seeing a film.

The image in the mirror moved in closer and closer to the palace and we saw the gardens spreading out on either side of us, to the right and to the left. There was a willow tree, and a bamboo bridge over a lake, and on the other side of the bridge there was a summer-house with a curving roof. Carved all over it there were dragons.

The reflection grew larger and larger, as if the building was moving towards us and we were floating over the lake and in through the door.

But the inside of the summer-house wasn't very interesting. It seemed to be nothing more important than a shed where Abu Nazir kept his gardening equipment. There were sacks of manure, and some rakes, and scythes for cutting grass, and on the shelves round the walls there were stacked some pots with plants and a rather dirty looking old oil can. The dirty old oil can grew larger and larger and larger until it filled the whole mirror.

The penny dropped.

'Hey!' I yelled excitedly. 'That's it. That's the magic lamp. It *must* be.'

Lady Precious Pearl smiled at me ruefully. 'The Golden Dragon warned me that Abu Nazir was a tricky one,' she said softly. 'And the Golden Dragon, as usual, was right. We would never have found it though we searched the palace for a year. Who but a very cunning magician would dare to place his most valuable possession in full view, on a shelf in a gardener's hut, where it is seen a hundred times a day, yet no one recognizes it because it looks like a scruffy, rusty old oil can?'

The image faded. But the mistiness didn't clear away. Instead it deepened and I heard the sound of horns blowing from far, far away.

Sir Roland stiffened, and his eyes sparkled. 'The horns of Elfland are blowing,' he said huskily. 'My friends, we are honoured this day.'

The mirror cleared and I saw a lady all dressed in white standing in the centre. In her hands she carried a sword and the hilt was encrusted with jewels.

She was surrounded by the strangest collection of dryads, and spirits of earth, air, fire and water, though I didn't know that's what they were at the time. Benjie told me later.

The white lady walked towards the mirror, and then she stepped straight through it and into the room, and we all moved back rather hastily because all her capering, cavorting companions came flooding in right behind her.

Sir Roland stepped forward and went down on one knee in front of her. We all did the same though I peeped up through my eyelids because I didn't want to miss anything that was going on.

'Knight of Arthur Pendragon,' said the lady, 'knowest thou who I am?'

'Yes, lady,' Sir Roland replied in a low voice. 'Thou art that same Lady of the Lake who once bestowed upon Arthur a sword of wondrous design.'

I peeked up through my fingers again. So this is the Lady of the Lake, I thought to myself. And this is me, kneeling here and actually seeing the Lady of the Lake.

Her hair was a silvery white, yet her face was neither old nor young. It was ageless but very sad, as if she'd seen and suffered a lot of things in her time. I tried to remember where I'd seen a face like it before.

I couldn't remember. And then, suddenly, I realized that she reminded me of Mum when she doesn't know I'm looking at her and she's sitting by the bed in the half dark thinking her own thoughts.

I pushed it out of my mind and listened to what was going on around me again.

'Behold Excalibur,' said the Lady of the Lake, and she held the sword towards Sir Roland. 'Accept it from my hands.'

'Lady, I am not worthy,' Sir Roland said.

'No man is worthy,' she replied quietly. 'But it is yours, for a time, as it was Arthur's, for a time. With this blade alone can Abu Nazir be unbodied. Take it.'

She placed the sword in Sir Roland's hands and he kissed the blade and then stood up and slid it into the long scabbard at his belt.

'May I return it untarnished into your hands, Lady,' he said. 'And give me your blessing as I set out on this, my final quest. And may your greatness of vision my Liege Lord Arthur, and your courage Sir Lancelot, and your humility Sir Galahad be my invisible companions on this, my quest.'

'Now you must go,' said the Lady of the Lake, looking neither to the right nor the left. 'Your long stewardship of Camelot is ended, Sir Knight. Depart now and my blessing goes with you all.'

Sir Roland marched out of the door with his head held up very high and the rest of us followed on his heels.

In the outer bailey Sir Roland paused at the stables and whistled and a white horse came galloping towards him, its mane shaking and its eyes rolling, whinneying with excitement. The knight put his foot in the stirrup and swung himself up into the saddle. Then he held out his arm and pulled Lady Precious Pearl up to ride pillion behind him.

We tramped across the drawbridge in single file, but, as soon as we stepped on the ground beyond the castle, we heard a rumbling, so we stopped and turned.

The towers were cracking and falling, and flames leapt

up and out through the windows and the bricks slithered apart. The walls crumbled, the oaken beams crashed inwards, and we caught glimpses of the Lady of the Lake and her spirits of earth, air, fire and water, undoing the spells that had held the whole place together for so long.

Thunder and lightning write across the sky.
The epitaph to this most fitting death,
And then let enchanted Camelot fall and die,
To be nothing but a memory, a whisper in the mind,
Speaking of chivalry, courage and example to all
mankind.

We heard her voice chanting this spell and thunder and lightning did rumble and flash across the sky, lighting up our startled faces and then leaving them in darkness again.

'Come,' said Sir Roland, 'let us be on our way, my friends. Camelot is gone.'

He was silent all the way back across the wilderness until we reached the ark.

Mrs Noah was waiting with the animals, and she had cooked an enormous supper and that cheered him up. By the time the ark had swung round towards the open sea, Sir Roland was chatting to the animals and telling them all about King Arthur and tournaments.

Shadow's Diary – Interruption 6

I'm fed up! Sick to my back teeth with everything. I'll tell you why.

My master, Abu Nazir, is the most powerful magician in the world. He has only to pick up his magic lamp, rub it with his finger and out comes a genie to do his bidding. If Abu Nazir said 'Go and tear down the walls of a city', the genie would go and tear down the walls of a city. If he said 'Pick up the ocean and pour it all over the land', the genie would obey. So you can see that Abu Nazir is a very powerful magician; yet, with all that power at his command, I find he is also incredibly petty.

That night, after I'd watched Camelot Castle crash into the dust, I went off to bed but I couldn't sleep because I was so excited. At last I knew exactly where my master hid his magic lamp, because, of course, I'd been watching like a hawk when the Lady of the Lake came through the mirror, and I certainly didn't miss the bit where the mirror showed Sir Roland the exact and precise whereabouts of the lamp.

For once I agreed with Lady Precious Pearl. Abu Nazir was definitely a cunning old sorcerer because, never in a million years, and sometimes I feel as if I've been searching that long, never would I have thought of looking in the jasmine summer-house. I must actually have seen the magic lamp hundreds of times but, like everyone else, I thought it was just an old oil can of no particular value.

I couldn't sleep for thinking about it. So, at dead of night I got up and I crept stealthily down the stairs and out into the gardens.

The jasmine summer-house is at the other end of the lotus garden. Quite a walk really, but the moon was high in the sky and I can see in the dark so I didn't mind because, if I once got my hands on that lamp, I'd be master of the world and able to get my own back by turning Abu Nazir inside out and throwing his palace all over the mountains.

I tiptoed to the bridge. The jasmine summer-house was quiet and deserted. I had a good sniff but I couldn't smell anyone lurking about either. So far so good. I pulled up a couple of Abu Nazir's favourite plants, just to pass the time, and then I slunk silently across the bridge and stepped on to the smooth green sward in front of the summer-house.

I rubbed my hands together. I was within a few yards of the magic lamp. There was a soft, low growl from behind me and my purple hair stood up on end.

I heard the padding of feet and another growl. And then, would you believe it, from around the side of the summer-house there stalked an enormous hungry-looking tiger.

It roared and bared its fangs. Nasty sharp pointed fangs it had. It crouched, lashing its tail. Then it sprang straight at me.

I've never gone up to the top of a willow tree so fast in my life

The tiger reared up and scraped the bark off the tree in great strips, making the most unpleasant sound I've ever heard. It paced round and round the tree and I had to stay up there all night and it was an uncommonly cold night for the time of the year.

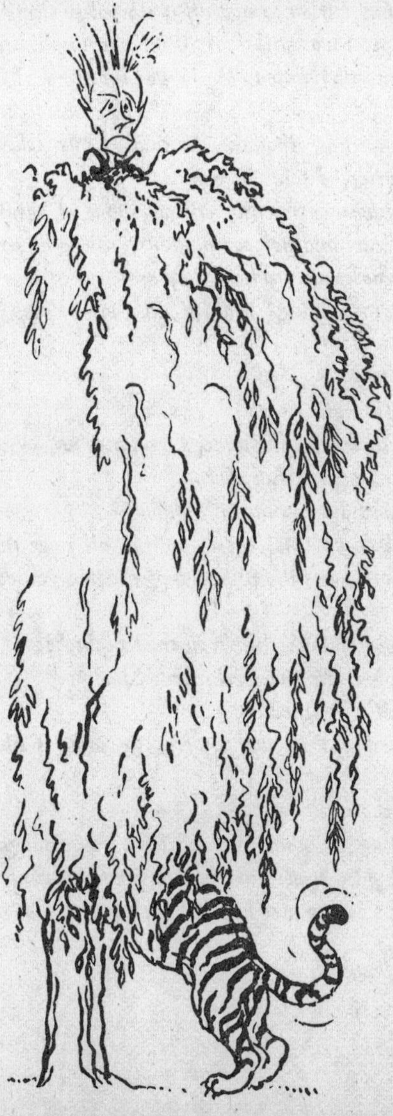

Every time I tried to nod off it started to climb up the tree, terrifying me. I was still there in the morning when my master came out into the garden. He looked up at me. I looked down at him.

'Good morning, Shadow,' he said. 'Lovely day, isn't it?'

'Yes, master,' I said. 'Lovely.'

'Time you went to the crystal room, I think,' he said. 'Precious Pearl and her companions will be at sea by now. I want to know exactly where they are.'

'I'd love to, master,' I said. 'But – er – y'see, I'm afraid of the tiger.'

He frowned.

'Tiger?' he said.

'Yes!' I shrieked, 'the tiger. Great big 'un. With teeth.'

He looked round, puzzled.

'Oh!' he said, 'you mean Tiddles.'

I looked down, and there, rolling all over the grass and looking idiotic, was the tiniest ginger kitten you ever laid eyes on.

'Tiddles only looks like a tiger at night,' said Abu Nazir. 'Have you been up there all night, Shadow?'

'Part of it,' I gulped.

He smiled. 'Well, well, well,' he said. 'Cold night too, wasn't it?'

I sneezed.

But you do see what I mean, don't you? Imagine putting a tiger in the garden at night just to prevent people looking for magic lamps in summer-houses. He's petty, that's what he is, petty!

8 The Stowaway

I was very tired after the long walk back from Camelot so I stayed in bed all cuddled up and warm and snug and listened to the sounds of the ark as it set out once again towards the open sea.

As you might have guessed it was the smell of cooking from Mrs Noah's galley that finally roused me out of my bunk to see if I could coax an extra large helping out of her.

After I'd had breakfast I went up on to the main deck where everything was the usual picture of confusion.

Two of the baby elephants were washing it down with their trunks. They had a bucket of water each and they sniffed up a noseful apiece and then blew it out of their trunks at about 150 kilometres an hour.

Old Man Noah trotted between them as they were doing this and it wasn't exactly good judgment on his part. When you are hit in the middle by a jet of water moving at that speed, interesting results are bound to happen.

Old Man Noah doubled up like a jack-knife and shot backwards along the deck till he met the edge of Number One hold, whereupon he turned a complete somersault and vanished down the hatchway without using the ladder.

'Of course,' he said amiably as he climbed out again and limped towards us, 'it is rather prejudicial to discipline when a ship's captain arrives at the bottom of a hatchway on his head but the only thing to do is to carry on as if that is the way you always descend into the hold. The only problem about that,' he added ruefully, 'is that it's rather difficult when you've just broken your neck.'

He sat down on a bollard and squinted up at Benjie. 'And now,' he said, 'can you answer me one small question? Which way do you want me to point the sharp end?'

'You mean the bows.'

'I believe some eccentric people call it that,' nodded Noah.

'East, south-east,' said Benjie. 'We are going towards the Kiangsu Mountains in ancient Cathay for that is where Abu Nazir has his palace and that is where we shall find Lady Precious Pearl's magic lamp. I'll show it to you on a map in the charthouse.'

'What on earth is the use of a map?' said Old Man Noah. 'All the maps I've ever seen are smothered in lines with silly numbers at the end.'

Benjie threw his eyes heavenwards and bounced his exasperation all over the deck. 'Those are the lines of longitude and latitude,' he explained. 'They show you the difference between where you are and where you are going.'

Old Man Noah looked utterly startled at this piece of nautical information. 'Do they?' he gasped. 'Well I never did! Why didn't somebody tell me? I rubbed 'em all out.'

'I give up,' sighed poor Benjie.

Before there was a chance to go on with the lesson in elementary navigation there was a commotion on the well deck and Mickey, one of Noah's pet monkeys, came flying through the rigging on the end of a line and dropped to the deck in front of us with his teeth chattering and his eyes rolling wildly.

'Daddy Noah, Daddy Noah,' he gurgled. 'There's a stowaway on board.'

Old Man Noah scratched his head. 'Where?'

'In Number Two hold,' said the little grey monkey.

'Hmph!' muttered Noah. 'I must investigate this at once. How dare anyone stow away aboard *my* ark. Of all the cheek!'

He strode masterfully away across the deck, then stopped and turned.

'Did the stowaway sound dangerous?' he asked cautiously.

Mickey nodded his head till it nearly fell off.

'Very,' he said. 'I was terribly scared.'

'Ah,' said Noah, and stroked his chin. 'Would he – er – bite people, do you think?'

'I wouldn't be a bit surprised,' said Mickey.

'Ahem, you wouldn't wouldn't you?' said Noah.

He looked around the deck where an interested crowd had begun to gather. Lady Precious Pearl with Sir Roland at her side, and Teddy Bear, and most of the animals were all watching fascinated the outcome of this event.

'Y'know,' said Old Man Noah. 'It's a funny thing but if there's a ship's captain on the seven seas with a real dislike of being bitten, it's me. And if there's a ship's captain on the seven seas more likely to get himself bitten *than* me, I've yet to meet him.'

Sir Roland stepped forward.

'Shall I search out this miscreant varlet for you?' he asked. 'I have a sword shall make short work of him.'

'Goody,' said Old Man Noah. 'Number Two hold is over there.'

Sir Roland strode towards the hold and disappeared round the edge of the charthouse. I daresay we'd all have followed him to watch what happened, but Mookey, the little brown monkey, came dashing on to the deck from the other end of the ship, and his eyes were rolling and his teeth were chattering too.

'Daddy Noah, Daddy *Noah!*' he yelled. 'There's a stowaway on board.'

Noah patted him kindly on the head. 'I know,' he said. 'It's all being dealt with by the experts. The biffing experts. Sir Roland has just gone down into Number Two hold.'

Mookey looked as if he was about to have apoplexy.

'It isn't in Number Two hold,' he said agitatedly. 'It's in Number One hold. I heard him making horrible, ghastly noises.'

'Perhaps,' said Benjie as Old Man Noah looked from one monkey to the other, 'perhaps there are two stowaways aboard.'

'Good gracious,' cried Old Man Noah. 'I hope not. If this goes on they'll outnumber the passengers.'

'Here he is,' cried Mickey and Mookey and clutched each other and hid their faces.

And before our bemused eyes, a tall, wivery, wavery figure floated up throught the deck and stood there, playing mournfully on his flute. It was the Spook.

Sir Roland, having found nothing to bonk in Number Two hold, came striding on deck waving Excalibur and then stared at this unexpected addition to the ship's company.

'What are you doing here, Sir Spook?' he demanded.

The Spook looked sulky. 'Where else was I to go?' he replied. 'My semi-detached castle is now completely detached. The lady told me to follow you as there might be a little something I could do to help you on this quest of yours. I'm homeless now, aren't I?'

'Of course,' Sir Roland nodded. 'Enchanted Camelot is no more.'

The Spook sniffed. 'There's lots more, actually,' he pointed out. 'But it's all in lumps on the ground. Something to do with Merlin's magic and not a word about it in the deeds.'

'Captain Noah, I will vouch for this Spook. He is quite harmless.'

Old Man Noah nodded. 'Apart from his music which is lethal,' he said. 'However I welcome you aboard provided you don't frighten my animals.'

'Thank you,' said the Spook gratefully.

Then he wafted himself across the deck and wavered in front of Benjie.

'You promised,' he said. 'You promised you'd listen to my music. All of it.'

Benjie sighed.

'A bargain is a bargain,' he said. 'Let's go to the blunt end. The wind will blow it away.'

It didn't seem fair to leave poor old Benjie to suffer by himself, so we all went and listened and the Spook, delighted to have an audience, played his flute for three solid hours. It was terrible. He played us every tune he'd ever composed since he fell or was pushed out of the minstrel's gallery and each one was worse than the one before. I think he must have been pushed.

Benjie and I clapped politely at the end of his recital, and Lady Precious Pearl tapped her fan and Teddy pulled two big plugs of cotton wool out of his ears and I wished I'd thought of that.

And all the time, the ark sailed steadily across a wide open sea towards the ancient land of Cathay and the Kiangsu Mountains where the palace of Abu Nazir was hidden in a valley between the Tiger's Eye and the Brothers.

Shadow's Diary – Interruption 7

I peered down into the crystal and concentrated hard on the ark and gradually it appeared, bobbing along on the sea with the sun shining down on the deck and everyone enjoying themselves lazing around and sunbathing. I hate watching people enjoy themselves. Ugh!

'Where are they?' asked that cool voice from the doorway.

My master flowed into the room. I daresay he had quite a lot on his mind, what with a knight and an invulnerable sword on his track, but, as usual, he showed no sign of it and that is what worried me most about him. He's so impassive you can't read his thoughts.

'The ark is just entering tropical waters,' I said.

He nodded silently.

'She is getting too close. I think it is now time I used the genie. You've never actually watched me use the magic lamp, have you. Shadow?'

'No, master,' I replied humbly.

'I think it is time that I brought Lady Precious Pearl here to my palace where I can keep an eye on her. As for her friends, well – we'll arrange a storm and sink their boat. The genie is rather good at storms. One of his specialities.'

'Can I watch it?' I asked eagerly. 'Can I watch 'em all go guggle, gurgle and guggle as they drown?'

'Perhaps,' he said, and smiled thinly. 'It may be a useful lesson for you to watch what happens to those who try to steal my lamp.'

'Yes, master,' I said, and offered him a sickly smile.

He gave me a smile right back, but his wasn't sickly. It was cold and utterly merciless.

'Cats play with mice,' he said icily. 'I am something of a cat, as you may have noticed. But there comes a time when cats stop playing with the mice. They eat them.'

I shuddered.

With one slender finger he began to rub the edge of the magic lamp. All the time he'd been talking to me he had concealed it in his robe, but now he brought it out into full view. It still looked like an old, dirty, rusty oil can.

A wisp of smoke curled out of the spout and there was a noise like the sound of steam escaping from a blocked kettle. The smoke flowed upwards in a spiral and vanished out of the window. Abu Nazir walked out on to the balcony and I followed him very cautiously.

The spiral of whitish grey smoke built itself up into a huge figure standing outside the tower with its head touching the clouds and its feet on the ground far below us.

I gulped and swallowed my tonsils. I had no idea it was going to be that big!

The genie sat down on top of one of the mountains and leaned forward so that its huge head was only a yard or two away. There was the rumble and crash of avalanches in the distance. It was black – black as ebony, and its eyes were tightly closed.

'M-m-master!' I gasped. 'The genie is blind.'

'It is the genie of power,' he said. 'And power is always blind. I am its eyes, dear Shadow.'

'Your wish is my command,' said the genie, and the towers

and minarets of the palace shook like a jelly at the sound of his voice. 'To hear is to obey.'

'I have a task for you,' said Abu Nazir. 'I wish you to stir up a great storm, a hurricane, a typhoon and sink a small wooden ark that is sailing north, north-east towards the Kiangsu Mountains.'

'Is that all?' boomed the genie. It sounded disappointed.

'No,' said Abu Nazir. 'Before you sink it and send it to the bottom of the sea I have a delicate mission for you to perform. I want you to pick up one of the female passengers aboard that ark.'

'Master,' said the genie submissively. 'I am blind. Typhoons I can manage. Hurricanes I can stir up magnificently, likewise earthquakes, fires and floods, but I am not fitted for such a delicate task as the one you require of me.'

'This I know,' said Abu Nazir. 'And I will send my assistant with you and he will point out which of the passengers I want you to bring back here.'

I felt my stomach drop down into my sandals.

'Me,' I said aghast. 'Go with him?'

'It will keep you away from the jasmine summer-house,' said my dear master softly. 'Go. Bring Lady Precious Pearl to me and don't make any mistakes this time.'

The genie's hand curled round me and I squawked in sheer terror. So would anyone if they were picked up by a hand as big as a courtyard and whirled away up in the air before they had time to gather their wits.

'Glump!' I gurgled, and looked up at the genie's nails. They were long, curved and vicious, and every one was as tall as a church steeple.

I peeped down between the cracks in his fingers and felt dizzy. We were flying over the sea at a speed that made my lovely purple hair stream out behind me. I clung to the genie's finger and had to stretch my arms out wide in order to do it.

Far below I saw the ark sailing merrily along on the emerald green sea.

'There it is!' I yelled. I gloated. Everyone aboard was so innocently, so happily, enjoying themselves.

Lady Precious Pearl was in the bows of the ark and I saw her look up and point towards us. Old Man Noah pulled out his telescope and had a squint through it and then he ran round the deck shouting orders.

In a matter of moments everything was panic and pandemonium as the genie went to work, pulling up wave upon wave and hurling thunderbolts into the sea.

The ark tilted sideways and everyone fell head over heels into the scuppers. We swept like a black cloud over the ship. A gigantic green wave crashed down on the stern of the ark, splitting it like a peanut.

The genie ran his hand along the deck. A fat woman with round eyes and a red face poked her head out of a hatchway and shrieked, 'Noooooah! What are you a-doing of?'

The hand of the genie stretched out towards her and picked her up.

'Not that one,' I yelled.

I could imagine the look on my master's face if I went back to the palace with Mrs Noah as a captive instead of Lady Precious Pearl. I'd never live it down.

The hand of the genie had closed round her but, hearing my command, he dropped her down the hatchway again.

Ahead of me I saw Lady Precious Pearl clinging to the ratlines to prevent herself being washed overboard.

'Straight ahead, genie,' I yelled.

His fingers groped blindly, touched her, and then, as I yelled triumphantly, 'That's the one', closed round her and dragged her away sobbing and screaming.

Sir Roland tried to hack at the genie's fingers but he might just as well have tried attacking a mountain. Benjie and Kipper pulled at it with their fists and the little green dragon tried to burn it, but the genie flicked its fingers and sent the pack of them tumbling across the deck.

A thunderbolt hit the ark amidships.

'We're sinking,' I heard Old Man Noah wail. 'Ban the moats. I mean man the boats. Women and old men first. Oh bother!'

And the ark sank. Noah and all his animals were struggling in the water. The last I saw was Benjie's busby floating away with two small animals in it, and Teddy Bear trying to hold young Christopher's head above water, and then the genie whirled us up in the air and away towards the Kiangsu Mountains.

A white and shaken Lady Precious Pearl was rolled across the floor of the crystal room and she crouched at Abu Nazir's feet.

There was a hissing of steam as the column of smoke grew smaller and smaller, a wisp of whitish grey that disappeared obediently back into the spout of the lamp. The genie was gone. All that power and energy was once again locked back inside that small, insignificant looking oil can. But I was ever so glad to have actually seen it at work. It made my day that did. Definitely an experience.

My master looked down at his captive as she crouched in a somewhat dishevelled heap on the floor.

'We meet again,' he said.

She struggled to her feet and stood, swaying slightly. Her face was pale and her eyes were frightened, but trying to look defiant.

'Lady Precious Pearl you are both obstinate and self-willed,' said Abu Nazir. 'The sacred lamp of power is mine by right, not by theft. Those who are ambitious enough, or greedy enough to want to obtain it, must fight me and they won't succeed unless they are genuinely strong enough.'

His eyes flickered across the room to glance at me as he said this, and I felt funny inside, as if he was looking right through me.

'My game, I think,' he concluded.

Lady Precious Pearl struggled to speak. 'Game of chess is not won till checkmate is called,' she said hoarsely.

Abu Nazir sighed.

'You are very obstinate,' he said quietly. 'You have lost the game. Your pathetic little army of small boys, toy soldiers, pensioned-off knights and teddy bears has been destroyed. They've gone, sunk without trace.'

Her head drooped wearily.

'Poor Kipper and Benjie,' she whispered. 'And Teddy, Noah and Sir Roland. I've brought great misfortune to you all.'

'Yes, you have rather,' said Abu Nazir. 'But then, people with a lust for power always do bring misfortune on their friends. You should have thought of that a little earlier. Take her away, Shadow. There is a room prepared for her and she can meditate a while. It is one of my best – er – meditation rooms. Take her to the dungeon with the spikes, the one next door to the pit with the poisonous snakes.'

'I know the one,' I said eagerly.

I was delighted. In my opinion he was behaving as a wicked magician ought to behave, because the room with the spikes is a really first-class meditation room for pretty girls like Precious Pearl. Thoughts that are meditated upon in that room have a definite point. In the ceiling there is a grid of sharp spikes, and, once the ratchet on a wheel by the door is unlatched, the spikes descend slowly, day by day and hour by hour, and the helpless victim has to watch them descend until they pin her writhing body to the floor. She'd have plenty of time to think in the dungeon with the spikes.

I chuckled.

'Will you come quietly or do I have to drag you?' I said to Lady Precious Pearl.

She drew herself up and looked at me disdainfully.

'I'll walk,' she said.

I sniffed.

'Spoilsport,' I said. 'I'd have enjoyed dragging you.'

I clapped my hands for the guards and two of Abu Nazir's special bodyguards entered the crystal room and stood one on either side of our prisoner.

I marched down the spiral staircase of the tower and along the lower corridors of the palace till I reached the door that led down to the dungeons. I unlocked the door and the two guards held her down while I strapped her onto the floor in a harness that held her body rigid.

She stared up at the ceiling. As I went out I clicked off the lock that held the ratchet and iron wheels began to turn. Her eyes widened with fear as she saw the spikes emerging from the holes in the ceiling.

I slammed the wooden door of the cell, and bolted it.

'Hee, hee, hee,' I giggled happily. 'No one is going to rescue you, you know. They've all been drowned.'

Then I went back to the crystal room highly satisfied with myself.

Abu Nazir was standing by the window, looking out, and his face was as remote and as calm as ever.

'Got rid of that lot very neatly, didn't you, master?' I said

chattily. 'Sir Roland and his invulnerable sword – the lot – all in one fell swoop.'

His eyes surveyed me and I shivered. He has very strange eyes when you really look into them.

'The trouble with you, Shadow,' he said, 'is that like all shallow, malicious and cruel people you insist on counting your chickens before they are hatched. It is one of the reasons, although I'm sure you'll never see it, why none of your plans is ever crowned with success. Before crowing in future, make sure that they've really gone.'

He waved his hand towards the crystal.

'At once, dear master,' I smiled. Even his insults had no effect on me because I knew we were winning.

I crossed to the crystal but, as I stepped delicately across the room, I felt something under my sandal. It was smooth and very slippery and my left foot shot one way and my right foot another. I grabbed the table in order to steady myself and it went over with a crash. So did the crystal. It smashed on to the stone floor and it shattered into a thousand pieces. I stared down at it. I looked up at Abu Nazir. I gulped.

'It wasn't my fault,' I howled. 'I slipped. I didn't mean to do it.'

Abu Nazir looked at me and then he looked at the floor beside me.

'As the lady said, it isn't checkmate after all,' he whispered. 'She has blinded me. I can no longer see my enemies.' He bent down and picked up a small, ivory fan.

'That is what you slipped on, Shadow,' he said.

He went out, leaving me alone in the crystal room with an upturned table, a broken stool and a shattered crystal.

9 The Shipwreck

The last I saw of the poor old ark it was having a bad case of thunderbolts amidships and I don't remember much else because everything seemed to turn upside down and I bounced across the deck on the back of my neck.

I didn't have time to be frightened. I heard Old Man Noah yelling and Sir Roland was shouting something about 'God for King Arthur and hurrah for St. George', but it didn't make much sense at the time.

The sea swallowed me and I was too busy kicking and swimming and gurgling to think about anything very clearly. Someone grabbed me by the scruff of my pyjama jacket and hauled me upwards and I found myself staring at Teddy.

'Very tricky things, genies,' he said.

Benjie's busby went floating by with a couple of Noah's small furry animals in it, so I grabbed at it because I knew he'd want it. Teddy propelled me towards a part of the deckhouse that was bobbing on the water and Benjie came up alongside and we both scrambled on to it together. It rocked about a lot with our weight, but it was better than being in the water.

Benjie and I looked at each other solemnly. 'Take note Kipper,' he said. '*This* is an adventure.'

'Glug,' I replied. 'No need to rub it in Benjie.'

'Just so's you remember,' he said.

The waves broke open and Sir Roland came up sitting on the back of his magnificent white horse. He was waving Excalibur in the air, though what use he imagined it would be under the circumstances I can't think. An invulnerable blade is no doubt very useful when it comes to hacking varlets or puncturing holes in wicked magicians, but it isn't a lot of use in a shipwreck.

I stared round at the scene. Old Man Noah's ark was most certainly sunk, but, being made of wood, it was coming up in bits and pieces all over the ocean. A few yards away to my right I saw Mrs Noah grabbing Old Man Noah by that nightshirt thing he always wears and she pulled him out of the sea and on to some planking.

'Picked me up it did,' she bellowed in her loud, clear carrying voice. 'Picked me up, hefted me about a bit and then dropped me down a hatchway.'

'Yes, dear,' gasped Old Man Noah.

'Sauce!' she exploded. 'Then it went and took that toffee-nosed looking Chinese girl you're all so barmy about instead. Why should *she* have all the attention? That's what I'd like to know. Picking me up and hefting me about and then dropping me down a hatchway. Nerve! Don't forget if we see it again. You tell it – You're my 'usband.'

'Yes, dear,' said Noah.

The driftwood began to collect together with most of the survivors clinging to it and by the time we got around to check who was who and what was what, it was fairly obvious that we'd all come up to the surface one way or another.

Teddy was virtually unsinkable till he began to get

waterlogged, and he was the hero of the hour, swimming around and rescuing scared animals and sitting them on planks and saying, 'There, there' and 'Never mind' and 'If things don't get worse they must get better'.

So we were all safe, for the time being. But we were still in a pretty bad way because floating around with a lot of driftwood in the middle of a tropical ocean wasn't helpful to our quest and it certainly didn't get us any nearer to rescuing our kidnapped Lady Precious Pearl.

And of course we had to try and rescue her, that went without saying. We weren't going to let Abu Nazir and his nasty assistant get away with it, genie or no genie, not if we could help it.

We lashed the bigger bits of the ark together and then we had a pow-wow about it – a council of war, Sir Roland called it. From my point of view it was a bit like being back in the dungeon at Camelot again: lots and lots of suggestions, but none of them were very practical.

In the middle of it I saw Spooky drifting across the water playing his flute three notes sharp as usual. I nudged Benjie with my elbow.

'Nothing upsets old Spooky, does it?' I said. 'He can walk through walls and prance about on water so a little thing like a shipwreck doesn't disturb him at all.'

'No,' muttered Benjie. 'But if he plays "Many Brave Hearts are Asleep in the Deep" once more I'll bust something.'

'Hello,' said the Spook. 'Everybody happy?'

'Yes,' we all chorused.

'Good,' he said, and beamed at us. 'I think it's going to rain.'

Old Man Noah tugged his wispy beard. 'I don't like to cast aspersions,' he whispered to Teddy, 'but y'know,

Spooky's one of those people who turn up at a wedding with a bag of black confetti.'

'Thanks for the weather forecast,' said Benjie. 'That's all we need. Is everyone all right out there?'

'Yes,' said Noah, chiming in quickly. 'Are all my little animals safe?'

'Oh yes, yes, yes,' said the Spook. 'I told *them* I thought it was going to rain too. They were ever so interested.'

I hitched up my pyjama trousers and rang out the water. 'We shall have to eat soon,' I observed. 'I'm getting hungry right now. I read in a book that there were these men on a raft, or something, and they hadn't got anything to eat so they had to bang sea birds on the head with an oar and eat 'em raw.'

'If any sea bird is so ill-advised as to fly that low I suppose we could give it a whirl,' said Teddy. 'But it doesn't sound very appetizing to me.'

'I've eaten worse on campaign with Arthur,' grunted Sir Roland.

The little green dragon fluttered on my shoulder and I patted it gently.

'I can always cook them,' he piped. 'For where there is a dragon there is always hot buttered toast. Chinese proverb.'

'We'll bear that in mind,' said Benjie gratefully.

I felt something trickling down my ears, but I didn't take much notice of it at first because I was generally wet all over.

But it went on and on trickling so I screwed my neck round and saw that the little green dragon was crying to himself.

'What's the matter, little dragon?' I said.

'I have failed to save my mistress from Abu Nazir,' he

sobbed. 'Woe is me. How can I ever face my mother, the great Golden Dragon, when I am such a failure in life?'

'We've all made a mess of it,' said Old Man Noah soothingly. 'Look at me. I'm the captain of the ship and a captain is always supposed to go down with his ship. It's traditional.'

'But your ship didn't go down,' Benjie pointed out. 'It keeps on popping up all over the place.'

Old Man Noah looked round.

Ah, yes,' he murmured. 'I hadn't thought of that.'

He wrinkled his nose and shaded his eyes with his hand. 'I say,' he squeaked. 'What's that, over there?'

I followed the direction of his pointing finger and my heart did a somersault right up into my mouth. Less than a hundred yards away I saw dozens and dozens of triangular fins cutting through the water towards us.

'Oh crumpets!' I cried. 'This is too much. Everybody, get your feet out of the water. SHAAAAARKS!'

There was an undignified scrambling from near and far as everybody tried to get themselves up on to a plank or the mast or the dismembered rigging. Sir Roland's horse came up on to the deckhouse and nearly threw the rest of us back into the ocean.

And there we sat, our eyes riveted to the slow circling of those ominous fins.

Round and round they went, circling the wreckage, and the wake they set up caused all the bits and pieces to be driven inwards, bumping gently together while we clung like limpets to prevent ourselves being toppled into the sea.

'Don't let 'em upset you,' yelled Benjie. 'Hang on for dear life.'

One of the triangular fins sliced through the water and

came up a bare metre away. We all held our breath. The water broke and a large grey white face appeared and bobbed amiably in front of our noses. It wasn't a shark. It was a dolphin.

'Can we be of any assistance?' said the dolphin politely. 'We saw your ship go down and we dolphins, as you doubtless know, have an almost uncontrollable urge to go and help sailors in shipwrecks. Boys often ride on our backs and I daresay that teddy bears, toy soldiers and even ship's captains can ride on us if they really try.'

The dolphin raised its head and gave a shrill, bubbling whistle and two of its friends swam up alongside and bobbed up and down beside it.

'What about my elephants, and giraffes?' said Noah anxiously. 'They can't ride on dolphins.'

The leader of the dolphins stretched its mouth in a wide, rubbery grin. 'Have you not heard,' he said promptly, 'that we dolphins have an amazingly high intelligence? Higher than most humans as a matter of fact. The problem was considered while we circled round, and now it has been solved.'

The dolphin waved a flipper in an unassuming sort of way and I stared across at the wreckage and saw that his friends, whole shoals of them, were patiently taking ropes from the driftwood into their mouths and winding them around and over and below the scattered wreckage so that it became one big raft.

Sir Roland rose to his feet and scrambled across to assist them by cutting the ropes to the right length with his sword. So I was wrong, wasn't I? An invulnerable blade does have its uses in a shipwreck.

'Climb aboard,' said the dolphin, and I slid down the deckhouse and put my leg over its smooth, slippery back.

'Cling on tight,' said the dolphin. 'We will take or tow you to the nearest beach which happens to be at the foot of the Kiangsu Mountains. You were headed in that direction so I hope I'm right in supposing that it's where you want to go.'

Benjie clambered upon his dolphin and waved his musket about triumphantly.

'You supposed just right,' he said. 'Watch out, Abu Nazir, 'cos we're on our way to clonk you a tuppenny one.'

'Hooray!' we all yelled.

The dolphins fanned out into a crescent formation and began to speed through the water and within a couple of hours we saw the tips of the mountain peaks rising above the sea. Within another hour the gentle arc of a yellow beach reached out its arms towards us and the helpful dolphins took us right up into shallow water from which we could easily wade ashore safely under the lee of some white cliffs pockmarked with caves.

'Thank you very much indeed,' I said, and shook my dolphin by the flipper politely.

'Ho yus,' said Benjie. 'Thanks to one and all from one and all.'

'Our pleasure,' said the leader of the dolphins modestly. 'If there is any little thing we can do, we always do it, for we know that we pass this way but once! Farewell and good luck.'

We all stood on the beach and waved goodbye to the dolphins while the rest of the castaways stumbled ashore.

The little green dragon flew across the sand.

'It is obvious,' he announced in the tone of voice he used when about to launch into a proverb, 'that to those

to whom luck is granted, destiny intends success. I am much heartened by that proverb.'

Benjie scratched his nose.

'I'm sure you are,' he grinned. 'But I'll tell you what I'm much heartened by. I am much heartened by what is coming out of that cave behind you. Somehow I didn't think those dolphins turned up just by coincidence.'

I swung round and so did the little green dragon. We both gasped. From out of the largest cave in the cliff there stepped a Golden Dragon, the sunlight flashing along its scales.

'Mother!' squeaked the little dragon, and flew towards her.

'Greetings, my son,' said the Golden Dragon. 'And greetings to all of you, O illustrious wayfarers. Now is the time for you to turn defeat into victory. For the first time in many years, all signs and portents are in our favour.'

The Golden Dragon bowed towards us. We all bowed back – well, most of us bowed. Benjie saluted, very smartly. Sir Roland drew his sword and waggled it about in a dignified manner and I managed a sort of non-commital nod because I feel soppy trying to bow.

'I s'pose you are Lady Precious Pearl's dragon?' I asked diffidently. It seemed a bit cheeky to ask such a question but I like to be sure.

'Indeed I am,' said the dragon politely. 'And now if you will come into my cave you can rest before setting out for your final battle with Abu Nazir.'

'Oh goody!' I cried. 'That means we are going to win, doesn't it?'

The Golden Dragon looked at me very steadily.

'No,' it said quietly. 'It means you have every chance of winning but we immortals may set you a task, we may even equip you for it, but you have to achieve success for yourselves and every battle is always a *real* battle.'

We followed the dragon into the cave feeling a trifle dampened.

'Eat and rest,' commanded the Golden Dragon. 'Mrs Noah will stay here with the animals but I want Benjie and Teddy and Noah to come with me to the palace. You also, young Kipper, and, of course, my little green dragon who can burn down the cell where his mistress lies imprisoned. In addition I shall require the services of the bodiless one from the nether world.'

Spooky looked round, very startled.

'Do you mean *me*?' he asked incredulously.

'Yes,' said the Golden Dragon. 'For there is a task to be performed that only you can perform.'

'There,' said Spooky. 'I always knew I had talent.'

Shadow's Diary – Final Interruption

'Tee, hee, hee,' I cackled. This was my big chance. I could feel it in my bones. Everyone in the palace was dashing about hither and thither like an ant's nest stirred up by a big stick. My master Abu Nazir had too much on his mind to worry about little old sneaky me, and ever since I broke the crystal, I'd had nothing to do except plot and plan to get my hands on that magic lamp.

I'd just seen Abu Nazir going down the stairs to his secret room in the west wing. I don't know what he does down there but he usually stays there at least a couple of hours working on his spells. I knew he had plenty to think about too. The palace was buzzing with rumours about dragons, and knights on white horses, and all the usual exaggerated nonsense with half a grain of truth in it. The way was clear for me to fulfil my ambitions.

There was the jasmine summer-house, in broad daylight and not a soul in sight. I crouched down behind a rhododendron bush and wondered if Abu Nazir really suspected that I knew where he hid the magic lamp.

I shivered a bit at the thought that he might know my nasty little plans because I've worked with him for long enough to know that it isn't very wise to try outwitting him. The results could be very unpleasant for the outwitter who failed.

I took a deep breath and decided to risk it. I crossed the bamboo bridge and hid behind the willow tree. No tiger. Good.

I dashed to the verandah of the summer-house and stood there, poised for instant flight. Not a sound. The door was less than a metre away and all I now had to do was find a way to unlock it. I was fairly sure that Abu Nazir had put a very strong binding spell on it, but I was a specialist in binding spells myself.

I gloated. There it was, a mere metre away. All I had to do was open it, step inside, grab the lamp, rub it and yippeeeeeeee, Abu Nazir and his palace would be whirled away into the middle of next week.

Something tapped me lightly on the shoulder. 'Hop it. Scat. Buzz!' I said, and brushed it away. Something tapped me on the other shoulder – heavily. I sagged, then turned round to see what it was.

It was a gorilla – a rather large one!

'Yaaaaargh!' it said, and opened its mouth wide so that I looked right down its throat. It had very big tonsils.

I don't suppose you've ever stood outside a Chinese summer-house on a fine clear day within a metre of becoming master of the world, and then found a huge, hairy gorilla rolling its bloodshot eyes at you. But I'm sure you can imagine my feelings.

'Oh – er – hello gorilla,' I said. 'I was just taking a little walk in the gardens. Flowers are very fine for the time of the year, don't you think?'

'Grrrrroooooogh!' it said, and began to beat its chest with its outsized paws.

'Very nice to have met you,' I said.

I stepped back a pace or two. The gorilla stepped forward a pace or two. He opened his mouth and hot foetid breath struck me in the face. I recoiled. The gorilla didn't.

'Heeeeeelp!' I shrieked, and ran for it.

I jumped for the willow tree and climbed hand over hand up to the top. The gorilla swung himself up and sat on the branch beside me.

'Yaaaargh!' it said, showing its gaping red mouth and yellow teeth. It meant business.

I screeched and dropped down out of the tree. So did the gorilla. I ran across a clearing and jumped over the back fence. So did the gorilla. I ran through the kitchen, across the yard and out into the front stables. So did the gorilla. I ran across the lotus garden, jumped over a wall and dived into a ditch full of leaves. So did the gorilla – same ditch, same pile of leaves.

I thought I was safe, but I wasn't.

Raising my head I came eye to eye with the wretched creature.

'Grrrrrgh!' it said nastily.

'Yeeeeow!' I said.

I fled. I pelted round the palace walls. I scaled a gateway, I swung on a clothes line, I rushed up the steps and back into the palace. So did the gorilla. I hurled myself through the door of Abu Nazir's throne room. So did the gorilla.

I jumped on the flying carpet.

'Up, up, up!' I screamed. Wrong carpet! The gorilla beat its chest. I beat a retreat. He grabbed at my fluttering robe. He got a handful of robe but nothing at all of me.

I ran through the conservatory, the library, the music room, the ballroom, the orangery, down the west terrace corridor and up the east terrace corridor, the living rooms, the greenhouses and the observatory. So did the gorilla.

I arrived back in the throne room and had another wild and frantic look for that flying carpet. I saw it and I jumped on it.

'Up!' I cried. 'Up, up, up!'

The whole of my past life flowed in front of my eyes in those last few seconds. I could find nothing, but nothing with which to reproach myself and that is what seemed so unfair about it. Not a day of my life had passed in which I hadn't been consistently mean, petty, malicious and vicious, so why was this happening to me?

The gorilla shambled across the floor towards me, breathing heavily.

'Fly, dear carpet, fly!' I yelled.

Slowly, sluggishly it rose in the air.

'Up!' I howled. 'Faster you idiot.'

The carpet shot up and left me hanging from the chandelier.

Then it went back to fetch the gorilla.

'No!' I shrieked. 'Not him. Only me. Come back at once.'

Would you believe it? That wretched carpet dithered about as if it really didn't know what to do for the best.

'Meeeeeeee!' I said. 'Take me at once to my room in the tower or I'll pull out your pile thread by thread.'

You have to be strict with them you know. It rose up beneath me. I sank on to it and it took me gently and carefully through the closed windows and up to the tower. I fell off it, sobbing with relief.

Abu Nazir was standing by the window looking out across the mountains. At his feet there was a large, hairy gorilla skin. He kicked it gently with his toe as I climbed off the carpet.

'Some people don't listen, do they?' he said. 'I thought I told you to stay away from the jasmine summer-house, dear Shadow?'

'I wasn't, I dud-didn't. I mean – I was just taking a lamp in the garden. I mean a walk in the garden,' I stammered.

Abu Nazir turned away and looked out of the window again.

'There are rather a lot of avalanches in the mountains today,' he said reflectively. 'I think the Golden Dragon and her friends must be on their way.'

'If you say so, master,' I said, still dizzy from my exercise and the sudden way he changed the subject.

'I do say so,' he said. 'And I think we shall find ourselves under attack before nightfall. Go to the walls of the citadel and make sure that all the sentries and all the guards are on full alert.'

'Yes, master,' I said.

I bowed low and staggered out. I told you he was petty, didn't I? At a time like that to go changing himself into a gorilla so as to chase me all over the palace!

10 The Golden Dragon

I was woken up by somebody shaking my shoulder.

I opened my bleary eyes and yawned. 'Go 'way,' I mumbled. 'Having a luvvly dream.'

'Wake up!' said a voice in my ear. 'The Golden Dragon awaits without.'

'Without what?'

'Without you at the moment, Kipper. Come on.'

I sat up and saw Benjie standing in front of me so I scrambled to my feet and followed him out of the cave and into a chill cold morning where I found Old Man Noah, Teddy and the little green dragon waiting for me. Spooky drifted through the side of the cliff and practised a run of tootles on his flute. The little green dragon was sitting on a rock practising huffs and puffs.

I yawned and stretched and scratched myself. I was still half asleep. I didn't notice the Golden Dragon crouched down on the yellow sand of the beach until Benjie walked up and saluted. 'Greetings, O Golden Dragon,' he said awkwardly. 'We are now all present and correct.'

Poor old Benjie! He is definitely out of place when he has to deal with any of the 'Big Ones', as he calls the immortals.

I stood on one foot and decided I wanted to get one problem settled once and for all.

'Excuse my asking,' I said, 'but whenever Lady Precious Pearl talks about you she calls you a "she" but when I think about great big powerful dragons I naturally think of you as a "he". Which way round are you, actually?'

'I laid the egg from which the little green dragon was hatched,' said the Golden Dragon gently. 'Do you know of *any* male creature that lays eggs?'

'Oh,' I said.

And that settled that.

'Climb on my back,' she said. 'The time has come for you to set out and rescue Lady Precious Pearl.'

'What about Sir Roland?' asked Benjie.

'I shall bring him later when you have rescued Precious Pearl and retrieved the magic lamp of power,' said the dragon.

Old Man Noah cleared his throat. 'Mrs Noah and the animals will stay here in safety?' he asked. 'You – er – wouldn't rather I stayed behind and Mrs Noah came with you? She's much better in battles than I am. Got a natural talent for it. She has a way of handling a rolling pin that puts fear into the stoutest hearts, I can assure you.'

'You are not going to be in a battle, my friend,' said the Golden Dragon patiently. 'Leave that to the biffing experts. You are going to use cunning, that's all.'

Benjie scratched his nose. 'A mere nothing,' he said. 'Just invade Abu Nazir's palace and rescue Lady Precious Pearl and then snatch the magic lamp. Do that twice before breakfast.'

'Quite so,' said the Golden Dragon. 'And now climb on my back at once.' When dragons talk like that you don't argue. You obey.

The Golden Dragon spread her wings and began to beat the air and we rose slowly but surely up into the cold, clear, morning air.

'We're going for a ride on a dragon,' I whispered in Benjie's ear. 'Isn't this fun?'

He sniffed.

'Ho yus, ever so,' he muttered. 'We've also got Abu Nazir waiting at the other end of the trip.'

The dragon banked sideways and started to fly north. The mountains dropped away beneath us. So did my stomach.

For an hour we flew faster than the wind and then I saw the high walls of a citadel, the curved rooftops, the towers and the minarets of Abu Nazir's hidden palace and we began to glide slowly, silently downwards.

We landed outside the walls in the deep shadow cast by a sycamore tree.

'Good fortune attend you,' said the Golden Dragon. 'I leave you now to accomplish your part of the task. I will return carrying Sir Roland on my back so he can challenge Abu Nazir to combat.'

The Golden Dragon smiled briefly down at us and then she rose in the air and vanished. You wouldn't believe anyone that big could disappear in a wink and a nod, but she did. There was a moment of flash and dazzle and by the time we'd finished rubbing our eyes the dragon had gone.

We were alone. Benjie scratched his nose yet again. Then he pulled it. Then he twisted it like a lump of plasticine and let it unwind itself back into its natural shape.

'Ho!' he said. 'Likewise ha! Didn't stay very long did she?'

Teddy Bear grunted.

'The Big Ones are rather like that I've found. I assume, however, that we do have sufficient brains, brawn and talent to accomplish the task or she'd not have brought us here.'

Benjie looked dubious.

'Wish I agreed,' he said. 'We are outside the walls of Abu Nazir's palace and we have to get inside the walls. Once inside we can't wander about dressed as we are, because a Teddy Bear and a soldier in a scarlet jacket, a small boy in striped pyjamas and an old man in a flannelette nightshirt are liable to cause gossip around the place, and Abu Nazir isn't a fool.'

Benjie went into his nose twirling routine again.

'What I want,' he said at last, 'is a couple of metres of rope.'

Old Man Noah looked up. 'Funny you should say that,' he said. 'I just happen to have a couple of metres of rope.'

Benjie looked astonished.

'You do?'

'I do,' said Old Man Noah. 'When I was a young man I was told by an authority that every ship's captain ought always to carry a bit of rope and I have dutifully carried a bit round my waist ever since. From that day to this I've never found the slightest use for it. Here.'

Old Man Noah hauled up his nightshirt and handed Benjie the end of a length of rope, then he revolved on one foot till it unwound itself. After that he fell over because he was dizzy.

'Kipper,' said Benjie to me. 'You and Ted go and lurk in those bushes over there and hang on to this end of the rope. When I say pull, tug like billyho. Got that?'

'Yes,' I said. 'But why?'

'Never mind why,' he grunted. 'Just do it.'

He took the other end of the rope and tied it round the trunk of the sycamore tree.

'Spooky. Job for yer. D'you see the gateway in the wall down there with those three Chinese sentries lounging about?'

'Yes,' said Spooky.

'Go and do your melting through the wall act round the corner here, out of sight, and then bob up and scare the daylights out of 'em from the inside of the palace. Make 'em run this way. Got it?'

'I daresay I can manage that,' said Spooky. 'But melting through walls is only one of my minor talents you know. I'm a musician really.'

'Mebbe we'll find a use for that later on,' said Benjie. 'Go to it Spooky.'

I peeped round the trunk of the sycamore tree and I saw Spooky vanish through the wall on this side, and then he re-appeared behind the sentries, flapping his arms and making grisly faces.

'Whoooo! Whoooo!' he moaned.

They swung round, yelled in panic and then ran straight towards our hiding place. Teddy and I pulled the rope as Benjie gave the signal and all three sentries tripped up and went flat on their faces and rolled over and over, the breath knocked out of them.

Benjie stepped out from behind the tree and pointed his musket at them.

'Halt or I fire,' he said grimly. 'Friend or foe?'

'We're friends,' they chanted in unison.

'That's your hard luck,' said Benjie. ' 'Cos I'm an enemy.'

We marched our prisoners into the shadow of the rocks and there Benjie made them take off their uniforms and Teddy and Noah tied them up and gagged them.

The little green dragon sat on a rock and looked down at them very fiercely. 'Anyone who tries to move will have their pigtails burnt off,' he said, and puffed out some flames to show them he meant business.

They rolled their eyes and looked terrified.

A few minutes later three rather peculiar looking sentries in Chinese costume marched through the gate-

way doing their best to hide a large brown bear until we reached the safety of some nearby rhododendron bushes.

Benjie grinned at me.

'You look like a fugitive from the Chinese Salvation Army.'

'So do you,' I giggled.

'Well, let's hope we can pass at a distance,' said Benjie. 'That's target number one achieved. We are inside the walls. Y'know what? Old Man Noah looks the most genuinely Chinese of the lot of us. It suits him.'

Benjie was quite right. Dressed up in the sentry's uniform, Old Man Noah did look like one of those old Chinese gentlemen who walk down the streets of Peking taking a bird for a walk on the end of a piece of string. I've got a picture of one in my encyclopedia.

Old Man Noah grinned happily. 'You likee?' he said. 'Me velly good Chink Chink Chinaman.'

The Spook rose up from the middle of the rhododendron bush and waggled about. 'What next?' he said.

'Target number two,' said Benjie. 'You must find Lady Precious Pearl and lead us to her dungeon. We'll hang about here and wait for you. When you find her, tell her that help is on the way.'

'Bye for now,' said the Spook and slipped silently away again.

'Ted,' said Benjie. 'You can't come with us. There's no way we can disguise you so I want you to get across to the jasmine summer-house and climb up the willow tree we saw in the mirror of Merlin. Your job is to watch out and see to it that no one gets that lamp. Got it?'

'I've got it,' grunted Teddy Bear. 'Carry on, Corporal.'

Teddy turned away and was just about to clamber up into a tree when he paused and turned round again and looked at Benjie very earnestly. 'Just between you and me and anybody else who is listening,' he said, 'you're working this out rather well, Benjie.'

Benjie grinned briefly, and the worried crease between his eyebrows smoothed itself out for a moment. 'Thanks, Ted,' he said gratefully. 'It's what is known as deploying yer forces ter the best advantage. I wish I didn't 'ave ter carve 'em so thin and spread 'em about so wide. Off yer go and keep yer eyes on that summer-house but don't try tackling Abu Nazir on yer own, will yer?'

'I won't,' promised Teddy, and then he placed his paws on the trunk of the tree and climbed smoothly out of sight.

I'd forgotten that tree climbing is as natural to a bear as breathing. Old Ted was completely at home in a tree and his brown fur blended with the branches so, in a few minutes, I couldn't see him any more.

I looked at Benjie with a new respect. 'Where did you learn all this?' I whispered.

'I'm a soldier, ain't I?' he replied briefly. 'It's what bein' a soldier is all about, Kipper.'

'I thought soldiers just bashed people,' I said.

'Hooligans bash people,' Benjie replied. 'Soldiers use tactics, my lad. Strategy, that's what. And strategy is the art of applying the exact amount of force to move a given situation, as my dear old sergeant used ter say. Hooligans apply violence and nearly always lose. Lotta difference between a hooligan and a soldier.' He sighed. 'I just wish I 'ad a little more force to apply, that's all.'

We stayed crouched down behind the bushes and waited for Spooky to return from his reconnaissance trip. The little green dragon curled itself up into a ball on my lap.

I felt fidgety and restless and I itched and I wanted to sneeze and I also wanted to get up and run into the palace and rescue Lady Precious Pearl with a few quick flourishes of my hands, but I knew there was no hope of that. So I waited. And waited. And waited.

I looked back the way we had come, towards the gateway and the high walls, and saw a tall figure in a silver cloak and a black turban standing by the ramparts, quite still, looking out across the plains.

'Abu Nazir,' I whispered to Benjie.

It was strange actually to see him after all this time. I shivered. Benjie patted my hand.

'He's looking fer dust,' he said softly.

'Dust?'

He's chosen a very good place for his citadel, high up in the mountains overlooking the plains,' said Benjie. 'And the Great Khan's army can't cross that plain without kicking up a dust cloud a mile high, so Abu Nazir will know when they're coming. No way are they gonna take him by surprise.'

'Oh,' I said.

'I've found her,' said a sepulchral voice a few inches from my left ear and I nearly jumped out of my skin. Spooky had at last returned.

'Where is she?' said Benjie.

'In a rather nasty dungeon on the right-hand side of the palace, below ground. There are some very sharp spikes about ten centimetres off her chest and she says to please hurry as she isn't at all enthusiastic about them and they are getting lower and lower.'

The little green dragon uncurled itself from my lap.

Benjie stood up. 'We're sentries coming off duty,' he said. 'Stroll very casual like but don't let no one get too near as I don't think this fancy dress will bear a very close inspection. Come on.'

We strolled out on to the pathway.

It was difficult to see Spooky in broad daylight but we followed him along the path towards the right-hand terrace of the palace.

There were a few people moving about here and there but they all seemed to be occupied with their own affairs. Servants were rushing about on their domestic errands, and a group of girls wandered past us but didn't take any notice of us so we gained the shelter of the side wall of the palace without being challenged.

Spooky went through a narrow door. We opened it and filed inside and found ourselves in a long corridor. We tiptoed down it until we saw a narrow, dark flight of stairs leading downwards and Spooky signalled that we had to go down them.

Just as we reached the top a large, lumpish man with a bunch of keys at his belt came plodding up. The little green dragon froze against the wall and looked for all the world like one of the ornamental dragons that were carved, here and there, all over the palace.

Benjie marched straight on and the lumpish man nodded as he passed.

'Prisoner's quite safe,' he grunted. 'I've just checked.'

Benjie nodded abruptly and plunged down the stairs. I followed, my heart beating like a demented drum.

Old Man Noah tripped and fell down the stairs and dropped his telescope with a loud clatter.

'Bother!' he said.

The jailer stopped, turned and peered down at us.

'Watch those steps, soldier,' he said helpfully. 'The third one is badly worn. I nearly fell down there myself.'

The jailer nodded affably at his fellow sufferers and then plodded away down the corridor.

'Blimey!' muttered Benjie. 'I thought he'd spotted us fer a minute. I've just swallered me Adam's apple and bitten the end off me tongue.'

The little green dragon flew over our heads and down the long line of cells to where Spooky hovered, waiting for us to catch up.

'She's in here,' Spooky said. 'But how you're going to get her out I really can't imagine. She is frightfully strapped up and pinned down.'

'Tell her we're here,' said Benjie.

The Spook flowed through the doorway and I wished it was going to be as easy for us, but obviously it wasn't.

'This is where you do your bit,' said Benjie to the little green dragon. 'All the huff you've got, matey. I want that door burned down and I want it fast.'

The little green dragon drew itself up, and then huffed and puffed, and puffed and huffed.

Flame streaked out and licked the wooden doorway. Smoke began to fill the passage way and the smell of charred wood caught the back of our throats and made us cough.

The door crackled and burst into flames and Benjie used the butt end of his musket to break open a panel large enough for us to scramble through into the cell.

Lady Precious Pearl looked up as we crawled in through the gap, and there were tears of relief in her eyes. I didn't blame her. Iron spikes were just a few centimetres off making very nasty holes in her body.

'Wind 'em back, Kipper,' said Benjie. 'That wheel over there.'

I saw the wheel and knew what I had to do. I've got a mechanical mind and I understand machinery instinctively, though I say it myself. Ever since I was little I've liked undoing watches and unscrewing electric light plugs and all that sort of thing. Dad thinks I may be an engineer when I grow up.

I pulled the ratchet lever and started to turn the handle. Behind me Lady Precious Pearl screamed.

'That's the wrong way,' howled Benjie.

I looked round. The spikes were now a centimetre off the end of her nose.

I turned the handle the other way very promptly and the spikes began to rise up in the air again.

By the time I'd got them back up to the ceiling and locked the wheel so they couldn't start coming down again, Benjie had unstrapped Lady Precious Pearl and she was standing rather shakily on her feet trying to get rid of the cramps and the pins and needles in her legs.

'Thank you, thank you,' she sobbed, and then she

flung her arms round Benjie, and Old Man Noah. She also kissed me, and it wasn't bad.

We crawled back through the hole.

'Now what?' asked Old Man Noah.

'Now,' said Benjie, 'you are going to do your star turn.'

'Me?' said Noah. 'I haven't got one.'

'Ho yus you have,' said Benjie. 'You, and Spooky – where *is* Spooky? Spooky!'

The Spook drifted out from the cell next door.

'I say,' he said. 'There's a pit full of poisonous snakes in there.'

'Yer don't say,' said Benjie.

'But I *do* say,' beamed the Spook. 'And you'll never guess. They *like* my music. I played to them and they danced about like mad. An audience that appreciates me, at last!'

'I'm very 'appy for yer,' said Benjie. 'And you can come back and play 'em your entire repertoire – later. At the moment we're still in the thick of it. Where was I?'

'You were about to explain to me my unsuspected speciality,' said Old Man Noah politely. 'And since I didn't know I'd got one I am bursting with curiosity.'

'Chaos and pandemonium,' said Benjie. 'That's your talent, Noah. You and Spooky between you. Little green dragon, I want you to make lots of fire and smoke while Old Man Noah and Spooky rush upstairs shouting that the palace is in flames and we'll do our best to creep out unnoticed during the ensuing confusion.'

The little green dragon nodded and went to work and Old Man Noah gathered up the hem of his uniform and rushed up the stairs yelling.

We plunged out after him through the smoke and the

flames and saw everyone in the palace rushing about like demented spinning tops.

'Fire!' yelled Old Man Noah. 'Run for your lives.'

They ran.

'The palace is on fire!' yelled Old Man Noah. 'Get water and put it out.'

Another lot ran to get water.

Spooky floated in and out crying, 'Whooooo! Whooooo!' and people who were running one way, promptly turned and ran into people who were already running the other way.

And, in the midst of all this panic and confusion, Benjie led Lady Precious Pearl out of the palace and into the gardens. I followed close on his heels and in a few minutes Old Man Noah, Spooky and the little green dragon joined us.

'And that,' said Benjie, 'accomplishes target number two. All we gotta do now is get hold of the magic lamp.'

'Benjie,' she said. 'You're marvellous!'

And she kissed him again.

'We 'aven't finished yet,' muttered old Benjie, looking very pleased with himself all the same. 'If yer goes on like that me head'll get swole and I won't be able ter put me busby on.'

There was a line of rhododendron bushes leading away across the gardens to the very edge of the bamboo bridge and the jasmine summer-house, and the useful thing about rhododendron bushes is that they have a sort of hole down the middle. We crawled inside and then walked down the long, dim tunnel of dark green leaves and branches, and no one could see us at all. At the end we stopped and had a look round.

The bamboo bridge over the lake was only a few feet

away, but we'd have to cross it in the open air and in full view.

'I hope Teddy made it,' murmured Benjie in my ear. 'Noah, you go first, then Lady Precious Pearl, and Kipper and me will bring up the rear. Climb up into the tree and don't drop your telescope.'

Old Man Noah scrambled out and walked up to the bridge. Halfway across he stumbled and we all caught our breath again, but he didn't fall over. Two helpful hairy paws came down out of the tree and hauled him up out of sight. Ted was there waiting for us.

Lady Precious Pearl slipped quietly out of the bushes and crossed the bridge without incident.

'Now, you and me as a cuppla soldiers strolling airily round the garden,' said Benjie.

We marched towards the bridge and we were about halfway across when we heard hurried footsteps behind us.

We shot across that bridge like two streaks of galvanized lightning and up into the tree where we sat on the lower branches and prayed that nothing was sticking out.

The footsteps came closer and closer. Then a thin, scraggy figure with a green face and pointed ears and purple hair came creeping stealthily into view. He wore a cloak with bat-wing sleeves and although I'd only seen him once before, disguised as a hermit, I recognized him easily enough. It was Shadow, Abu Nazir's assistant.

He stood in front of the summer-house and chuckled and rubbed his hands together.

'My last chance,' he said aloud. 'My master will be here to get the lamp so I *must* get that door open.'

He cleared his throat and made some peculiar passes in the air with his hands.

'KEEPER OF THE SEVENTH KEY!' he chanted.
'OPEN WIDE THAT DOOR FOR ME.'

Nothing happened. The door of the summer-house remained tightly closed.

'INFERNAL DOOR WITHOUT A KEY.
OPEN, OPEN SESAME!' he yelled.

The door still remained closed. Shadow bit his nails and danced round in frustration. There was a rustling noise from over my head and I saw Teddy Bear drop silently to the ground right behind Shadow.

'Hrrrrmph,' said Teddy.

Shadow spun round.

'Oh Nooooooooo!' he yelled. 'First a tiger, then a gorilla, and now a bear. It isn't fair! I hate everybody!'

'Grrrrr!' said Teddy and jumped towards him.

Shadow shrieked and ran across the bridge. Teddy Bear dusted his paws and climbed back into the tree.

As he settled his bulky body against the crook of a branch I heard bugles ring out from beyond the walls, and looking up I saw the Golden Dragon circling the palace in full view with Sir Roland mounted on its back, brandishing Excalibur so that the sword flashed in the sunlight.

'Sir Roland is here,' I cried. 'And we haven't got hold of the lamp of power yet!'

We all looked at each other in dismay.

11 The End of the Quest

It was clear that we had to move very fast if we were not to fail at the last moment.

We scrambled down out of the willow tree and we all converged on the summer-house and stood staring at the door.

The Spook came wandering over the bridge in his ethereal fashion and joined us.

'Anything I can do to help?' he asked.

Benjie rubbed his nose.

'Pop inside and make sure it's there?' he suggested.

'Make sure that what is there?' asked Spook.

Poor old Spooky! He didn't really know what the quest was about because no one had found time to explain it to him.

'Just go inside and see if there is a lamp in there,' said Benjie.

The Spook shrugged his spectral shoulders and obligingly dissolved through the walls of the summer-house.

'Yes,' he called. 'There's a lamp in here. It's hanging from the ceiling and has a perfectly dreadful shade all round it. Whoever chose it has no taste at all.'

Benjie opened his mouth to yell at him that that wasn't the sort of lamp we were looking for when we all heard footsteps approaching the bamboo bridge again so we jumped for the willow tree and scrambled up into the branches in somewhat undignified haste.

Shadow came running on to the patch in front of the tree.

'I don't care,' he was saying passionately. 'I just don't care any more. Tigers, gorillas, bears, the whole menagerie. I *won't* be thwarted. I won't. I won't. I *won't*!'

The Spook drifted casually back through the walls and the two of them stared at each other.

'Who are you?' squeaked Shadow.

'Me,' said the Spook, 'I'm a ghost, of course. What did you think I was?'

Shadow bit his fingernails.

'I recognize you now,' he muttered. 'You were the wretched Spook who let 'em all out of Camelot Castle when I'd locked 'em up in a deep, dark and dismal dungeon.'

'That's right,' said the Spook.

Shadow twitched his batwing robes agitatedly. 'And that means the rest of 'em are around somewhere,' he said. 'They didn't get drowned after all. I don't care. You hear me. I don't care! She shan't have the lamp. No one is going to have the lamp but me, me, *meeeee*! So there.'

'I'm not stopping you,' said the Spook. 'But I'd certainly change the shade if I were you. It's awful!'

Then I saw a tall figure in a silver robe and a black turban moving towards us from across the gardens. Lady Precious Pearl saw it too and her fingers clutched mine and her nails dug into me so that I almost yelled. Girls have very sharp nails.

Desperately I looked back at Shadow who was still standing in our way.

'My master is coming,' he moaned. 'I *must* open that door but I've tried every opening spell in the book and it won't budge.'

'You've tried 'em all?' said the Spook.

'Yes, all of 'em,' groaned Shadow.

'Then in that case I can tell you what's wrong,' said the Spook happily. 'It isn't locked.'

'*What*!' shrieked Shadow.

'It isn't locked,' repeated the Spook as if he was talking to an educationally sub normal child. 'There is nothing in the world so calculated to baffle a robber as trying to unlock a door that isn't locked in the first place.'

Shadow's jaw dropped open.

'Do you think my master is such a fool as to leave the door unlocked so that anyone can just grab the handle, turn it and walk in like thiiiiiiiis – it's *open*. Leaping Beelzebub, it's *open*!'

And sure enough it was.

Shadow jerked the handle and almost fell into the summer-house.

We jumped down out of the tree, determined to rush him as he came out, but a cold wind suddenly seemed to turn our bones to jelly and we all of us stopped dead as a figure crossed the bridge towards us.

'No,' I gasped. 'You shan't stop us!'

And I found myself standing alone in front of Abu Nazir.

'Don't look at his eyes,' I heard Benjie yell, but it was too late. His eyes looked into mine. I couldn't move. I couldn't breathe. I couldn't escape. I looked into an abyss.

The magician's eyes widened and grew bigger and bigger and the dark brown turned to fire and then to ice and I stared into Abu Nazir's world and into Abu Nazir's mind.

I can't tell you what I saw. I can't explain it. But I never want to see it again as long as I live.

'Stand aside, small one,' he said coldly. 'You cannot fight me. Don't try.'

And then his eyes flickered away from me and I stumbled back and Teddy and Benjie put their arms round me.

There was a howl of glee from the summer-house and Shadow re-appeared, holding in his hand a small, rusty looking oil can.

'I've got it,' he said. 'I'm master of the world and I've beaten you all. Votes for Shadow!'

Abu Nazir didn't move. He stood there, quite still.

'I wonder how long you'll keep it?' he said amusedly. 'I'm afraid the genie can't be released quite as easily as you imagine, dear Shadow. Nothing is that easy.'

'I shall keep it forever, master,' said Shadow. 'And you will be my slave.'

And it was then that I saw what was amusing Abu Nazir so intensely, for, perched on the wooden rail by the door, looking like one of the carved dragons on the summer-house there was a dragon that wasn't carved at all.

The little green dragon reared up its head, puffed out a stream of flame and burnt Shadow on the wrist.

'Wow!' cried Shadow, and he dropped the lamp and the little green dragon caught it.

Two seconds later it was in Lady Precious Pearl's hands

and the dragon was perched on her shoulder to make sure that no one took it away again.

'My game, I think,' she said quietly.

Abu Nazir surveyed her as calm as you please.

I have to admit that he was a cool one that magician. He didn't leap about or flap or get flustered.

Abu Nazir was defeated, yet he still dominated all of us.

He bowed very slightly, and his lips twitched. 'I concede you the game, Lady Precious Pearl,' he said. 'But I shall return. You will have to release the genie if you wish to stop me and I doubt if you can, as yet. Try, by all means, but, in the meantime I don't think that a small boy, or a moth-eaten Teddy Bear or your little toy soldier are quite strong enough to prevent me escaping. Farewell.'

He turned and walked back across the bamboo bridge. There he stopped. The Golden Dragon came sweeping down out of the sky and barred his path and she wasn't going to move aside.

Behind Abu Nazir there was his palace, in flames. He stood at bay.

He drew the long curved scimitar from the scabbard at his side and made it whistle through the air.

'You have a champion, of course,' he said to the Golden Dragon.

'We have a champion,' she replied.

Sir Roland stepped out.

'Behold Excalibur,' he cried. 'On this blade is written your final defeat, Abu Nazir.'

'Only if you are quick enough and strong enough to pierce me,' said Abu Nazir contemptuously. 'You have been long out of practice Sir Roland, gazing into mirrors in your enchanted castle. Your methods are as out-dated as those of the dinosaur. If I win, I go free?'

Sir Roland nodded sombrely.

Abu Nazir smiled faintly. 'I might have known you'd play by the rules,' he said.

His scimitar swept down in an arc and blood spurted from Sir Roland's wrist. It was his sword wrist. Excalibur dangled uselessly from Sir Roland's right hand.

There was a groan of dismay from Teddy and Benjie and Noah, and I didn't feel too optimistic myself at that moment.

'The fight had not started,' said Sir Roland indignantly.

'Mine had,' said Abu Nazir simply.

The scimitar was moving again and Sir Roland had to back away fast, dropping his shield and transferring Excalibur to his left hand.

I was biting my knuckles and, beside me, Lady Precious Pearl began to breathe very fast. Her index finger hovered over the lamp. I could feel her dilemma. Should she use the lamp? Should she release the genie? Or should she let the fight continue to whatever the end might be?

Sir Roland was in pain. He stumbled back. He *was* out of practice.

Abu Nazir moved like the wind. He darted forward, then back. He dipped and weaved and feinted first with one hand and then another, and at each move a little splodge of blood appeared on Sir Roland's body. On his arms, on his chest, on his face. And always he seemed to be retreating. He had an invulnerable sword that would neither break nor lose its edge but he wasn't swift enough, nor his reactions fast enough to use it.

Round and round they circled. Sir Roland fell. He tripped, stumbled and fell, rolling over and over to dodge the swiftly biting blade of this opponent. He staggered to his feet and stood there, swaying.

Lady Precious Pearl caught her breath in a sob.

'I *must* use the lamp,' she cried, and she began to rub it but nothing came out except a tiny little wisp of smoke.

She stopped rubbing.

'I haven't the strength,' she cried. 'I haven't the strength.'

Sir Roland was being driven back and back towards the bamboo bridge. He moved like an old man and I saw, for the first time, that he was indeed an old man. The enchantments of Camelot no longer held him in their timeless grip and there was grey in his hair and lines of deep weariness and fatigue in his face.

The fight was taking it out of him, of course, but there was something else the matter with him. Abu Nazir was using his scimitar with the speed and precision of a streak of lightning, but he was using his tongue too. He was talking softly, insistently as they wheeled round and round each other on the grass.

We couldn't hear what he was saying. Mocking and sneering, I supposed, the way people do when they want to throw you off balance and make you lose your temper. I have a friend at school who does that whenever we play table tennis and it's horribly effective.

Spooky moved in front of me and raised his flute to his lips.

'Get out of the way,' I shouted. 'You're blocking my view.'

But he took no notice. Instead he blew into his flute and I heard the sound of a bugle call. It was the 'Advance'.

And we all saw Sir Roland's back straighten and strength seemed to flow back into his arm as if he was remembering the pennants of King Arthur fluttering in the wind at Baden Hill.

'Arthur!' cried Sir Roland. 'God for King Arthur and England!'

And he flung Excalibur out of his hand, straight at Abu Nazir and it struck the magician in the chest.

For a moment Abu Nazir rocked back on his heels and then he stood still. He looked incredulous. It was the one move he'd never expected because it left Sir Roland unarmed if it failed.

We saw the scimitar drop from his fingers and a most extraordinary expression crossed his face. It was almost exultant.

'You have won!' he cried, and his voice reverberated like a bell. 'And I, at last, am free!'

He fell.

We all rushed forward, shouting and cheering and then, as suddenly, we stopped. There was the sound of a mighty wind and something black and icy cold swept formless across the sun, and for a moment the sun darkened as if it was in an eclipse.

Then it cleared. The sky was blue again. Sir Roland picked up Excalibur and poked the black and silver robes that were outstretched on the grass. He lifted them up on the blade of his sword.

They were Abu Nazir's robes all right, but there was no longer anyone in them.

'The quest is ended,' said Sir Roland to Lady Precious Pearl. 'You now hold the lamp of power and the burden of it is yours.'

Lady Precious Pearl bowed her head.

'I know,' she said. 'It is not a light burden.'

You'll never guess what she did then. She burst into tears. Girls are the strangest creatures.

12 Home for Christmas

It was all over and we were the triumphant victors in the quest. For five days there was great rejoicing and feasting and merrymaking for one and all. Mrs Noah and the animals came to the palace from the cave and she was so pleased to get away from boiling things up on an open fire she excelled herself by cooking the most delicious food. At the end of all the jollifications we assembled on the terrace of the palace and Lady Precious Pearl said goodbye to each of us in turn.

She kissed old Benjie and his ears went red.

She shook hands with Teddy. 'Look after them all,' she said.

'What else?' said Teddy gruffly. 'I'm one of the guards, am I not?'

I saw Old Man Noah arranging all his animals on a series of flying carpets ready for take-off while Mrs Noah re-arranged them the moment he'd got them settled. Life was going back to normal.

'Goodbye, Kipper,' said Lady Precious Pearl. 'I know I'm only a girl and therefore useless but remember me sometimes. And take this. It is an ivory statuette that I've had specially carved for you. Otherwise your mother will be short of one Christmas present.'

'Thanks,' I said, and stuffed it in the top pocket of my pyjama jacket. 'You're not going to kiss me or anything soppy like that are you?'

'No,' she assured me.

'Good,' I said.

'But, before you go, I have a special present for you. Behold, one little green dragon who wishes to go home with you.'

I beamed. I felt my face split open into the biggest possible grin. I held out my arms and the little green dragon flew towards me and let me actually cuddle it for a while.

'Cor, thanks, smashin',' I said. 'Are you sure?'

'I hold the lamp of power,' said Precious Pearl. 'And that is protector enough for the time being.'

The little green dragon blinked its golden eyelids up at me. Obviously it was about to give birth to another Chinese proverb. It did.

'I am a gift of great value,' it piped, 'because gifts of greatest value are those which give themselves.'

She waved and we all waved back as the carpets rose in the air followed by the rest of the convoy, and then the palace was just a pattern of oblongs and squares far, far below.

But we still had company. Flying alongside was the Golden Dragon, her scales glittering and flashing as her wings beat the air.

'Farewell, small ones,' she said. 'Farewell.'

So it was all goodbyes, which was sad, in a way, yet in another way it wasn't because we were on our way home and we'd be there in time for Christmas.

For the first time it struck me that Lady Precious Pearl looked rather lonely standing on the steps of the palace and waving us goodbye. She had got what she wanted I suppose . . . But I was glad I was going back to my attic room.

There was one more farewell before we got home.

It came as we flew towards the Midnight Mountains.

We were crossing the forest of Carbonek, and I was staring down at it because I'd only seen it briefly by night on the voyage out, when I became aware that the carpet was dipping towards land. We flew over the treetops at branch scraping height and a huge, pale blue lake opened out in front of us quite unexpectedly. The lake was fringed with high reeds, yellow and deep green, and the water was quiet and still. There was something breathless and uncanny about the lake, but it wasn't an evil place like the forest. It was peaceful and all over and around it there was a silence. The lake wore the silence like a cloak.

The carpet landed and Sir Roland stepped off and stood alone on the shore.

'Lady of the Lake!' he called and it seemed to me as if the reeds picked up his voice and repeated the message to the water for ripples began to revolve across the lake to its very centre.

'Lady of the Lake,' said the reeds.

'Lady of the Lake, Lady of the Lake,' echoed the ripples.

'Behold, I return Excalibur untarnished into your hands,' said Sir Roland.

He whirled the great sword round his head three times and then flung it out across the water. An arm clothed in white came up out of the water and a hand caught the sword, waved it three times in return and sank down again beneath the ripples.

We watched the silver glint of it as it descended down and down into the depths.

A mist rolled across the surface of the lake and I knew something else was about to happen because this one wasn't an ordinary mist. It moved and twisted and swirled about and finally took shape as a stately silver ship that moved silently towards us.

It was crammed from stem to stern with lords and ladies and knights. Sitting under the awning on the poop deck there was an old king with a golden crown, and beside him, three queens with silver crowns. And on the awning there was emblazoned a red dragon.

'The red dragon of Arthur,' said Sir Roland. 'Cousin to your Golden Dragon, my friends. The red dragon of Arthur came from China over the mountains of Tibet many, many centuries ago.'

I didn't know that. You live and learn, don't you?

Sir Roland turned towards us. 'Farewell, my dear friends,' he said. 'Tis time I went into Avalon, for behold, my Liege Lord Arthur himself has come to greet me, and all my old companions, Lancelot, Galahad, Bedevere and even surly old Sir Kay.'

He stepped into the water and it turned to ice and he walked across to the boat and hands came out to welcome him aboard. The ship became a drifting curtain of mist once more and we were alone on the shores of an empty lake.

I yawned. I rubbed my eyes and felt the carpet rising into the air but I don't remember crossing back over the Midnight Mountains.

All I remember is the voice of the Lady of the Lake saying, 'Wake up! Wake up Kipper! Time for school!'

'Coming, Mum!' I said, and sat up in bed.

Mum was smiling down at me and she really does look like the Lady of the Lake.

She dresses differently, of course. Be a bit of a sensation in the supermarket if she went out shopping dressed in long white robes after all.

'Time for school,' she said, and grinned at me.

'No, it isn't,' I shouted. 'It's Christmas Day. Where are my presents, Mum?'

'Breakfast, then church, and after that you can open your presents,' she said. 'You know the rules, Kipper.'

'Can I look at my stocking presents?'

She nodded.

So I grabbed my longest stocking which I'd hung at the end of the bed and I pulled out a Mars bar, some smarties, a lump of coal and a potato.

'Dad put those in,' I said. 'He puts them in every year. He isn't very original, is he?'

Then I dived down and found a paintbox, and some chalks and a box of those oil pastel crayons and then, right at the bottom, my fingers scrabbled at something else.

It might be one of Dad's jokes, or it might be something extra nice, so I dug my fingers down and pulled out a tiny green dragon and in its teeth it was carrying a most peculiar looking mannikin made of rubber. He had a green face and purple hair and wore a cloak made out of bat's wings.

'We thought he'd make you laugh,' said Mum.

I contemplated him thoughtfully. 'I wondered what became of him,' I said. 'But he isn't funny you know.'

'Isn't he?' she said. 'Daddy and I thought he was very funny.'

'You don't know him like I do,' I told her. 'He's

malicious, and cruel and spiteful and greedy, and he'll *never* learn. Still, thanks all the same, Mum. We'll control him somehow, Benjie, Teddy, Old Man Noah, and me. What's for breakfast and do I *have* to go to church?'

I crept up to the attic door after I'd eaten Christmas dinner, and I pushed it open a crack and peeped inside.

Teddy and Benjie and Old Man Noah were all of them sitting up on the window sill.

'Did you notice,' said Old Man Noah, 'that one of Kipper's presents was a balsa wood, do-it-yourself model of the *QE2*?'

'Lumme,' said Benjie vaguely. 'Was it?'

'Yes,' said Old Man Noah, and began to hum to himself.

Benjie looked at Teddy. 'Y'know Ted,' he said, 'the

thought of Old Man Noah as captain of the *QE2* is very sobering.'

'Hmph,' said Teddy.

I closed the door and left them to it and I went downstairs to start building my balsa wood, do-it-yourself model of the *QE2*.